Tales of the Terminated

A Humorous Look at Life After a Layoff

Tami Cannizzaro

Pink Dog Press
9206 Whitehurst Drive
Dallas TX 75243

For more information regarding special discounts for bulk purchases, please contact the publisher at info@pinkdogpress.com.

Book cover design and book design by goodmedia communications, llc

The text in this book is set in Times and BlackJack

Manufactured in the United States of America

Library of Congress Cataloging-in-Publication Data Available Upon Request

ISBN 978-0-9856902-0-5

To anyone who, at one time or another, ends up in the Land of Layoff. May this book provide inspiration and may you find humor on your journey.

Contents

PREFACE   7

ACKNOWLEDGMENTS   11

I'M SORRY, YOUR SERVICES ARE NO LONGER NEEDED   13
    Top 10 Good Things About Being Laid Off   15

IDENTITY THEFT   19
    It's 8 AM, Where's My Office?   21
    Do You Want Fries with That?   23
    Are Those Your Shoes?   26

CH-CH-CH-CHANGES   31
    Free Time Equals Freak Out Time   33
    Lessons from the Island of Misfit Toys   36
    Spirals and Pencils and Pens, Oh My!   40
    Hanging a Shingle   44

IT'S NOT YOU; IT'S ME   49
    Am I Dating or Am I Job Hunting?   51
    Did Etiquette Get Laid Off Too?   55
    Dangling Carrots   58
    Flattery: The Ultimate Recruiting Tool   61

DEBIT OR CREDIT?   67
    Vegetables: Are They Really a Necessity?   69
    Mail Call   72
    Financing a Layoff   76
    Am I Allowed a Spring Break?   80

HOME SWEET HOME OFFICE   85
    Woof! My Executive Assistant is Calling   87
    Is My Underwear Showing?   90
    I Love You. Now Please Leave Me Alone   94

MAKING LEMONADE   99
  Vikings and Margaritas   101
  Expecting the Unexpected   104
  The Cavalry Isn't Coming   108
  Winner, Winner, Chicken Dinner!   112
  Fear of Flying   116

LOVE IT OR LEAVE IT   121
  Acing the Test   123
  Going to the Show   127
  Dancing With Unemployment   130
  Nickels, Nickels, Nickels   133
  The Philosophy of Donuts   137

LIVE AND LET LEARN   141
  Friends Say the Darndest Things   143
  Climbing the Ladder   146
  Uno, Due, Cha-Cha-Cha   150
  Less is the New More   154

LIFESTYLES OF THE NOT SO RICH & UNEMPLOYED   159
  Card of the Year   161
  Driving to the Altar   164
  Off the Grid   169

OH CHRISTMAS TREE, HOW LONELY ARE YOUR BRANCHES   173
  Ho-Ho-Holiday Parties   175
  Holiday Meltdown   178
  Last-Minute Friends   182
  Things I Might Do If I had Time   185

WHEN IN DOUBT, WEAR A TIARA   189
  When Bad Fashion Happens to Good Interviews 191
  It's All Relevant   195

ABOUT THE AUTHOR   199

Preface

I never intended to be laid off. It was definitely not part of my strategic career plan. Even though I was working at a company that was clearly experiencing serious business challenges, I always hoped that it wouldn't be me when the pink slips started flying.

Truth be told, when the time came I pretty much knew I was on "the list." The company had experienced numerous layoffs during my tenure, and the business was struggling. My department had been eliminated a couple months earlier, and I was spared, moved to another department to work on "special projects." You don't have to be a rocket scientist to know that anytime your title says "special projects," it's a temporary gig, and you had better have your résumé together.

Mentally, I tried to prepare for my departure and my LAL— life after layoff. My immediate plan was to take a vacation—we already had the trip booked—and it would be a great way to kick-off this new chapter in my life. Once home, my goal was to keep as busy as possible. Rule number one: must be up, dressed and ready to go by 9:00 a.m. While I always looked for and applied for full-time work, my dream was to be a consultant. My list of to-dos included reaching out to all my contacts (thank goodness I'm a constant networker and this was not something I had to learn), join a networking group and do some volunteer work while I had the chance. With my action plan in place, my consultancy would take off or I'd find fulfilling work elsewhere. It never occurred to me that it would be anything but a smooth ride.

Something I didn't count on was the range of emotions that would envelop me as a result of the layoff. With my mind free from stress and distractions I was able to think about things and realized that there was a lot more to being laid off than simply losing a job. Stress, heartache, happiness, anger, sadness, boredom, loneliness, feeling less-than-successful—you name it, I felt it. And there was humor—yes, funny things happen when you've been laid off. Suddenly I had an idea: I would write a blog called *Tales of the Terminated: A Humorous Look at Life After a Layoff.* I figured if I had this wide range of feelings, others in layoff land probably did too. And just maybe they would relate to my stories and enjoy the humor I found during this journey through unemployment.

So I began writing some of my tales. Yet fear took over, and I put my writing away. After all, in my mind I was not really a writer, and I didn't want to open myself up to failure, especially after being laid off … until one snowy, icy day, when Hubby and I were stuck at home. I had read all the magazines in the house and was tired of solitaire. The cold must have given me a blast of courage as I pulled out my stories and decided to start my blog. Just like that.

The response has exceeded my expectations. People tell me they can relate to my tales and that I give a voice to what they are feeling and experiencing. The best part is that it has boosted my confidence, something that takes a beating when you're laid off.

This book is a collection of stories from *Tales of the Terminated*. They are based on my personal experience navigating through my life after the layoff. Some stories are funny—after all, I can find humor in almost any situation. Some are more poignant. Some are lessons to be learned. All express the range of feelings and emotions that came with being laid off.

The tales are mini-stories; enjoy reading them in any order you choose. In fact, it might be more fun that way. However you choose to read, I hope you enjoy them and maybe laugh a bit. At the very least, I hope this book shows that, if you've been laid off, you are not alone on this journey. We're all in this together. And it's not all bad. As my friend Steve used to say, "There's always a silver lining."

Thanks for reading,
Tami

Acknowledgments

My heartfelt thanks to all who have encouraged me through this journey of unemployment, job search and writing. To Val, one of the smartest women I know, who inspired me to chase my dream. To my vast network of family, friends and colleagues who have showered me with support and hundreds of coffee dates. A special shout-out to the PRCs—you know who you are. You were the first people with whom I dared to share my writing; thanks for your encouragement. To anyone who, as an unknowing participant, provided inspiration for my tales. To my executive assistant who listens while I read my tales out loud, showing support with barks and wags of approval. Most of all, thanks to my wonderful hubby. Your love and support has given me the courage to take this leap of faith.

Oh, and I guess I should thank the company for laying me off. That was a good decision—at least for me.

I'm Sorry, Your Services Are No Longer Needed

Top 10 Good Things About Being Laid Off

It's been a year. Happy Anniversary to me! Yay me! Sort of.

Hard to believe that one year ago I was laid off. Yep, walked out the door with my box of office accoutrements, ready to discover the new super-awesome opportunities awaiting me.

My mind was reeling with possibilities for the future. Maybe I'll be a successful entrepreneur. Or I'll be courted by tons of companies all wanting to hire me. Or maybe I'll travel the globe on business. Lose weight! Get abs of steel!

Hmmm ... twelve months later and I'm still considering the possibilities. And no abs of steel either.

If you had asked me a year ago, this is not exactly how I thought things would have turned out.

Good news is that the last year was actually pretty great. While I have had my down moments, I'm not sorry for the experiences the layoff has provided. Aside from the lack of steady income, there is so much to be thankful for: good health, great husband, my dog, home, family, friends, etc.

Top 10 Good Things About Being Laid Off

10. Cooking. I'm not the next Top Chef, but now that I actually have some time I have discovered that I'm a pretty good cook who can experiment with food and create a good meal. Hubby is enjoying it too. So is Masud, our local pizza guy, and our "go to" when my dinner creation is, well, not so good.

9. Exercising. Now I can go to the gym any time of day. No more rushing in for a 10-minute workout just before they close the doors. Although I have wondered, who *are* all these people at the gym in the middle of the day?

8. Hobbies. There's plenty of time to rediscover hobbies and complete half-done projects. Okay, so I haven't really completed my projects. I have made an attempt. At least the projects are now organized in the closet. Sort of.

7. Reading. Aside from reading multiple books this past year, I now get the luxury of reading a newspaper—cover to cover. Did I mention every day?

6. Coffee. Having time to sit and enjoy my morning coffee at a table instead of balancing it in a moving vehicle while navigating traffic is heaven, as is meeting my friends and business colleagues for coffee, meeting recruiters for coffee, and working on my laptop at Starbucks with—you guessed it—coffee. Apparently drinking coffee is a requirement for being laid off.

5. Vacation. The-Best-Ever! Sure, I took vacations before, but work was always at the back of my mind. What's the saying? It takes

a week of long hours to prepare for vacation and another week of long hours when you return to catch up? Not this time, baby! It was nothin' but fun.

4. Thinking/Planning/Strategizing. What better time to uncover a great opportunity than when you can actually clear your mind to think? Be free to consider all the possibilities? Daydream if you want, guilt-free.

3. Reconnecting. The time to reconnect with family and friends has been priceless. Gotta make time for that in any future work schedule.

2. Volunteering. Need I say more?

And the number one Good Thing About Being Laid Off (drum roll, please) ...

1. The gift of time. Life after a layoff has provided the time for all the things listed above and countless other things that have filled this wonderful year. When do we ever get such an opportunity?

Sure, there's still the stress associated with networking, looking for work, wondering where my next opportunity will be, but getting laid off was far from the worst thing that could happen.

So if it happens to you, don't be afraid to really *experience* it and all that life after a layoff has to offer.

Gotta run ... time for another cup of coffee.

Identity Theft

It's 8 AM,
Where's My Office?

How did I get here? Who are these people? Why am I here? Is this a parallel universe for the unemployed?

Here, exactly, is a networking group. I know you've heard of such groups. Some of you have even been to one—I know because I've seen you there. Don't pretend you don't remember; I have your business card.

Those of us in career "transition" (don't you love this buzzword?) get directed to these groups once the layoff hits. So here I sit each week with 200 of my unemployed compadres listening, meeting, making small talk—trying desperately not to look desperate.

It's a weird cross between a pep-rally and an AA meeting. Each week participants introduce themselves to the group and ask for contact information or in some cases announce that they've found a job. "Hi my name is Tami and I'm a marketing/PR executive. I've been out of work for X months (ooooh), and I just accepted a job at X (ahhhhh)." Cheers and applause ensue, as well as a stampede by the group to get the scoop on how exactly you landed this job.

This happens every week. Same time, same place. The predictability of each meeting is killing me. So why do we do it? Because we need to feel like we're someone again, like we have a *place to go—* an office. Predictability is a good thing for most people, especially those still in shock from losing their job. Think about it—every day of our lives we have a routine called work. A job requires us to be there, to listen, to produce, to engage. Predictability reminds us of having a real job, some place to go to. Without the comfort of our office, we can get lost.

Sure, the weekly meetings include résumé services, speakers and of course the invigorating pep-rallies, but the real beauty of a networking group is realizing we're not alone in this journey. It allows us to make connections and new friends, and even re-connect with old acquaintances. We're part of a team again, and as we cheer for those who are moving on to the next opportunity, we realize that's going to be us one day.

So when I get up to give my speech, I expect to see everyone on his or her feet. Waving banners. Cheering until their voices are gone. And I'll do the same for them.

Better start practicing, because my turn's coming up soon.

Do You Want Fries with That?

Hi welcome to the store! How may I help you today?

It seemed like a great idea—taking a seasonal job at the mall, at the store where I started my career. My strategy: add structure to my weeks and provide a guaranteed way to get out of the home office and connect with society. Not to mention making money, although that can be debated—after all, the job came with a nice employee discount on purchases. A girl can always use a new accessory, right?

What a great feeling, being out and about. Having people rely on me to do a job. Being needed. Meeting people. And then the inevitable, running into people I actually know. I had tried to prepare for this, but pushed the thought to the back of my mind.

The first time it happened, it was one of my former co-workers. Entering my domain, she spied me quickly and approached. "Hi!" I said. "Great to see you." Then she gave me *the look*, you know, sort of a once-over that could only be interpreted as pity or that she was looking down her nose at me. She glanced around the store. "Oh, so you're working here now?" I bravely smiled, and asked how I could help her. We finished the transaction with small talk, promising half-heartedly to stay in touch. I wonder how long it was before she was texting others to say that I, a former director at a Fortune 500 company, was now working at the mall?

That night I went home in tears. Not because I was ashamed of my work; I loved this fun part-time job. But because it was another reminder that my identity was in question, teetering between "I was" and "I am," as I tried to reconcile these feelings.

No one can underestimate the uncertainty, the *lost* feeling that shrouds us, when we—dedicated career people—suddenly find ourselves without the comfort of our job title.

I will be the first to admit that I used to claim, "I am not defined by my job." Yeah, right. Who was I trying to kid? That is all I have ever been about—climbing the corporate ladder, working hard and loving every minute of it. Since I am without human children (my child has four legs and wears a fur coat), when the layoff came I didn't even have the option of slipping easily into the career of motherhood.

I do cherish my role as a wife and life-partner to the greatest man in the world, yet even he will admit that I am career-all-the-way. If we had children, he would be better suited to staying home with them than I would be. So yes, I am defined by my job.

The second time it happened, it was a boisterous group of women, out shopping and having fun. As fate would have it, one of them was a friend from high school. We did not even recognize each other until she presented her ID to complete the transaction. *Here we go again*, I thought, waiting for the pity glance. *Is this what my career has been reduced to, working at the mall? What's next? A promotion to fast food?*

This time, my friend, whom I hadn't seen in years, did what I couldn't seem to do myself. She stated who I am, regardless of job situation. She gave me confidence, gushing about my career and accomplishments like I was the epitome of career women everywhere.

"She's been high up in the company," she told her friends. "She's done this and this and this." I wanted to stop her and tell her friends that I really wasn't that high up in the company or as important as she made me seem. But I didn't. I liked hearing for the first time in quite a while that someone admired my career. Not once did she look at me with pity. Nor cause me to question my decision to work part-time. I could have jumped across the counter and hugged her to death.

Yes, I have worn the hat of a corporate marketing and public relations director. I also wear the hats of wife, daughter, sister, aunt, friend and part-time worker—all very important titles.

Hi! Welcome to my store! Are you back to purchase again? Yep, it feels good to be needed. Let me know if I can help you.

Are Those
Your Shoes?

Remember the college ritual of meeting someone new? The series of questions that were always asked: Where are you from? What high school did you go to? What's your major? Where do you live?

I used to get bored with these questions and would brainstorm new ones that I thought were more interesting: Are those your shoes? Does your mother know you're here? Has your nose always looked like that?

Okay, I never really used my new questions, but some days I really wanted to. Why did we ask the questions? It was an easy way to establish a person's identity. We could all relate to this information, categorizing each other in our minds: She lives on campus, majors in architecture. He's from Houston, engineering major, Memorial High School.

Once we joined the workforce, all of these informational questions were compacted into one short sentence: What do you do?

"I'm Director of Marketing," "I'm Manager of Accounts Payable," "I'm a teacher," "I'm VP of Finance." Usually each of these statements is followed by a more detailed description of the company we work for and what we actually do. It's all about establishing our identity.

What happens when we find ourselves without a job? How do we identify ourselves without the luxury of a title and a company name attached to it?

Aside from finding the next opportunity, this seems to be the biggest hurdle to overcome after a job loss. Answering the question, "what do you do?" is more difficult than it should be. It's easy to stumble, not knowing exactly what to say.

I've come up with some pretty rockin' answers for myself. In case you didn't know, I'm a racecar driver—IndyCar, of course. I happen to be the right size for this job, and no one can tell who's in the suit when you put the helmet on anyway. Or, just in case I'm with a race-savvy crowd, my answer becomes "I invented Ziploc® bags." And my backup plan for both of these: "I'm a secret agent currently working undercover in the unemployment market. Shhh … my work is top secret."

Don't steal these; they're mine. You'll have to come up with your own identity. Seriously, I know what you're thinking: *You're not identified by your job, there's more to you than work, you only work because you have to, etc.* We've all said these words at one time or another. It's not until we're faced with a job loss that we realize those words can be hollow.

Re-establishing one's identity is tough. It takes lots of thought and consideration. Just like any major brand, we have to determine who we are and what we stand for. Except we have to do this without a fancy job title or company name attached.

So how do you find your identity again? No, a superhero cape and mask are not the answer, although I imagine such a fine outfit would come in handy for job interviews.

One way is to imagine meeting yourself. Who do you want to be known as? Look at your résumé for inspiration; your experience counts here. Even if you're changing careers, there are words from your past work that can be used to describe who you are now.

Hi, I'm Tami. I'm a marketing and PR consultant and a speaker. I'm also a writer. And I mentor students.

Who are you?

Ch-Ch-Ch-Changes

Free Time Equals Freak Out Time

Ah … freedom! Freedom from the alarm clock, work, traffic, to-do lists and all those other pesky things that come with a job.

So *this* is what it's like to be laid off? Is all this freedom supposed to be fun? In the beginning, I'm filled with anticipation of all the fun that awaits me. I make a list of projects that I have been waiting to do, you know, until I got some "free" time. Clean the closets, organize the kitchen, paint the bedroom, read, take a class, scrapbook, visit with friends, etc.

Honestly, after a day or so all this free time is freaking me out.

Part of me knows that I need to take some time for myself to relax. But come on, I am used to going 90 miles per hour all the time. Do I even know what the word "relax" means?

So I consult a dictionary: "relax—to make or become less tense or rigid; to release from tension or anxiety." Yeah, right. Obviously, the person who came up with this definition hasn't met me.

My type-A personality insists that I immediately contact everyone I have ever met, develop a spreadsheet to meticulously track my job search, create unforgettable business cards, investigate working on my own, check every job board known to man for available openings, attend any and all networking events, volunteer, spend hours at the gym to get abs of steel, become a gourmet cook, make breakfast for my hubby every morning, take a road trip throughout the state to visit friends—*whew*! No wonder I'm tired and unfocused.

Clearly, I don't know what to do with all this free time.

Well-meaning friends and colleagues call with their recommendations as to how best handle the situation. Most insist that finding a new opportunity will be very difficult and that I need to start panicking right now. Okay, they don't *say* panic, but I can hear it in their voices. Like I really need to hear that finding a job will be difficult.

Do ya think I haven't thought about that?

A few brave souls share with me the secret that others either do not want to admit, or are too jealous of my free time to dare say: *It's okay to take some time for yourself.*

These layoff veterans tell me to take time for myself; don't spend all my time looking for work. Do whatever makes me happy. One friend planted a garden while she was looking for work. Another became reacquainted with the gym. Another spent time enjoying the nothingness for a change.

I'm trying out this new approach, although it is tough for me to be still and savor the peace while I have it. Yes, I have some worries, but nothing is so overwhelming that I can't take an hour here and there for myself. Will I plant a garden? Probably not, since it means getting my nails dirty. But I do see some clean closets in my future.

Lessons from the Island of Misfit Toys

Remember the TV story of Rudolph? He was bullied because of his red nose, basically laid off from the reindeer team, and found quirky new friends in gold hunter Yukon Cornelius and Hermey, the elf who wanted to be a dentist. Together the new friends set off to find their place in the world, ending up on the Island of Misfit Toys. I usually tear up at this point, seeing all the beautiful toys banished to a cold island simply because they had the misfortune to be unique instead of looking like the other toys.

I have always been thankful that I am not an outcast like the toys, and tell myself this is never going to happen. I am with the "in" crowd. No desolate island for me. Unless, of course, I become super wealthy and purchase a private island to use as a vacation spot.

Then I went to a networking event.

Suddenly I found myself attending a two-day seminar on interviewing skills, something I never thought I would attend. How I ended up there is still a mystery. Well, not entirely. I threw my business card in the bowl at a networking event and won the opportunity to be tortured—*I mean coached*—with a group of folks. *I am such a sucker for throwing my name in the hat to win a prize.* The intent of the seminar? To improve our interviewing skills. In front of a group of strangers. While the moderator filmed us. You call this a prize?

On day one of said seminar, I was not in the mood to be coached for anything. Even if they had promised I would be a supermodel by the end of the day, I wasn't having it. But I had committed, so I dressed in my finest interview attire and dragged myself to the event. Taking a seat at one of the tables, I scanned the room, eyeing the other participants. *Hmmm ... Seems like I've landed on the Island of Misfit Toys.*

There were lots of sad faces and frowns and bad combovers and mismatched suits. Maybe this is a different seminar? I checked my invitation. Sigh ... I was in the right place.

Why am I here?, I thought. *I'm not "one of them," am I?* My bad mood turned into self-pity and sadness. *Am I also a misfit?*

Until then I had thought myself a bit special—that I might be "above" the masses that had been laid off. But no, I was one of them. I considered the crowd: no jobs, résumés in hand, sitting in a room waiting to be told how we could improve ourselves. We were all a bunch of misfits! No one wants a Charlie in the Box!

The speaker began and as it turned out, the guy was engaging and funny. A few half-smiles dotted the room. *Maybe this won't be so bad,* I thought to myself. The seminar began; we went through a workbook of exercises interrupted by group discussions. I made it through the first day of torture.

Day two and everyone, including myself, seemed to have relaxed a bit. I was determined to make the most of my self-imposed torture. After all, I did put my business card in the bowl to "win" so I only had myself to blame.

Then reality hit—the filming! One by one we faced the group, looked into the camera, and told our story. We answered questions as though this were a real interview. The moderator stopped us frequently: "Watch your posture." "Look me in the eye." "Speak up; we can't hear you." "Start over again."

On and on this went. I actually saw sweat pouring from one participant's forehead. Poor guy. Someone call for makeup.

My turn already? Really? Isn't there someone else who should go ahead of me? It was like I could hear Rudolph's mean friends taunting, getting ready to laugh at me.

Deep breath; get it over with, I thought. I seemed to be doing well when the moderator stopped me. With complete conviction he told me what he thought my career should be.

I was stunned by this revelation. Without a conversation between us, he said something out loud that I had written down earlier in the day about my "dream" career. How did he know about this? Did he steal my notebook during the break?

There I was on the Island of Misfit Toys, and Yukon Cornelius had discovered gold in me!

Little did the moderator know that his career choice for me had been a secret passion of mine, one that I had been fulfilling through volunteer work. I had been afraid to voice this dream for fear of being laughed at—who wants to be a misfit *and* be laughed at? The moderator encouraged me with positive feedback. He pointed me in a direction that I never thought I could go.

I left the seminar with newfound confidence. Whether I decided to move forward with the new career or not, the possibilities for my career seemed endless.

You know what? It's okay to visit the Island of Misfit Toys—magic can happen there. Be careful, though, you might learn something.

Spirals and Pencils and Pens, Oh My!

This is it—the time of year I've been waiting for. As soon as I hear the "thump" of the newspaper on our porch, I am out the door to be the first to grab it. The edition is huge—Sundays are always like that.

I tear through the paper, looking for them. And finally—there they are. The styles this year are insane! Too many things to choose from; I'm going to need to pace myself so I don't spend too much.

Sipping my coffee, I look carefully through each flyer at the offerings. Lots of newness. I'm loving everything. What am I looking at? The school supplies ads.

Every year I get excited about the plethora of writing instruments, paper options and organizers. This year is no different. Right now I'm Jonesing for new colored pens and spiral notebooks.

I need more pens like I need a hole in my head. As I write this, I'm staring at three containers filled to the brim with an assortment of pens, pencils, markers and highlighters. And that is just on my desk. Don't get me started about the markers in my craft bag.

Crazy, isn't it? I've been out of school for years, yet I still get excited about this stuff.

Hubby shakes his head as I circle my choices in the advertisements. He knows that there is a trip to the French superstore, Tarjay, on my agenda. Oh, but he also knows better than to say one word to me about this little obsession of mine. He's even worse than I am; Hubby is a chronic pen stealer. Every day I find at least a couple new pens somewhere. They're everywhere—his car, the kitchen counter, the dresser, the coffee table. Yep, if we ever need to write something we have a pen for it. Periodically, we bag up these "foster" pens, and he returns them to his company.

Not sure where I got this obsession with all things back-to-school. Maybe it was the thrill of shopping, even if it was for necessities. Mom always set aside an afternoon to take us to get our supplies. We picked out coordinating binders, spirals and other accessories. Sometimes I managed to get my lunch box to coordinate with my notebook. Remember when colored notebook paper was the rage? And what about the Trapper Keeper? Those things were awesome!

Now that I think about it, I'm pretty sure it was more about new beginnings. The start of school signaled an opportunity to begin fresh. New classes, new friends, new activities—and yes, new pens. Newness was everywhere. New weather too, which also meant new clothes. But that's another story.

Funny that as we get older and more established in our work lives, we tend to forget about the newness that is fall. Unless you are a teacher, summer is nothing more than a hot drive to the office, which transitions seamlessly into fall. Nothing new.

Until a layoff hits. Then we are faced with a totally different version of new. It's new that we are no longer on a work schedule. It's new that our email accounts aren't flooded with incoming messages. It's new that we no longer have steady income. And it's new that what once stressed us out is what we crave the most—work.

One way of looking at a layoff is to focus on all things negative: no income, no job, no career advancement. Seems like some people are trying to go for the Guinness record for the longest pity-party.

My way of looking at a layoff is a bit different. Just like our school days, this is a chance for a new beginning. A new company, a new job, even a totally new and different career path. Just like we got to start over in school each fall, with a layoff comes the opportunity for a career do-over.

Many have told me that a layoff is not a happy time; I should be scared, I should forget about following my dreams and just find a job. Any job. Wow, talk about adding stress to my life.

These folks tell me I can start over at any time, once I have a job.

Really? How many people, busy in their career, suddenly decide to stop midstream to pursue something new? While I do know one person who did just that, for most of us that kind of courage is not in our DNA. It is against all that is rational to quit a job—with income—to just "start over," especially if it's the antithesis of our current job. For me, at least, it's counter-intuitive.

I know, I know. Many of us have financial obligations that require income. I'm right there with you. Yet I still see this as an opportunity. I'm going to grab the reins and do something that I really want to do while I have the chance. Something new.

These layoff opportunities don't come around often. At least I hope they don't.

Hanging a Shingle

I used to be fascinated with becoming a consultant in my field. I envied those who were able to step away from corporate life to work independently, managing multiple clients or moving from client to client, creating their own destiny. This seemed like such a glamorous role—somewhat entrepreneurial yet less risky. From my pre-layoff perspective, consulting did not seem to require a large amount of cash to begin—just tell your friends and colleagues and print some business cards. Ta-da! Instant consultancy!

The main point of intrigue for me has always been the aspect of control. If I was a consultant I'd have control over everything: my work life, my free time, decision making, budgeting. Power, baby!

Yet, despite all the positives I envisioned, I could never seem to take the leap of faith and walk away from a job with a steady income, health insurance, 401K and other benefits. Even during frustrating times at the office, I struggled with leaving the known for the unknown.

When I realized a layoff was pretty much inevitable, I began plotting—I mean planning—my LAL (Life After Layoff). This was an exciting time for me. The plan was to take a few days off and then begin my new venture as a marketing and PR consultant. My life was forever going to change—and in a good way. Being a consultant would create the flexible lifestyle I dreamed of: going to the gym, enjoying my pool, taking time for other interests—oh, and working. No more would I be a slave to the corporate clock or be controlled by "the man," whoever that guy is.

The first day of my new venture, I sat down at my computer. Hmm … where to begin? I almost drew a blank. Where did my business sense go? Was it accidentally turned in to HR along with my laptop during the layoff?

A name! Yes, that's it. What to name this new venture? Obvious choice is to name your business after yourself, which is more difficult than it seems since I also wanted to secure the URL. Who knew that my lengthy Italian last name would already be taken?

URL, hosting service, business cards—wow, when did these things get so expensive? Still, I pressed on.

As a marketer and strategic thinker, it seemed as though I should develop a business plan. Yep, never go anywhere without a roadmap. Several hours later, I still had a blank document in front of me.

Scratching that for a while, I put my serious marketing hat on and listed the tactics for getting the word out. I updated my LinkedIn account and emailed friends and former colleagues. That was easy enough. With my new business cards in hand and emails out, it was time to sit back and wait. Any moment now the work requests would start coming in. Yep, any minute now. Just a matter of time.

All I heard were crickets. And not very many of them chirped through the silence.

You know what all those "independent consultants" fail to tell you? It is hard to start out on your own. Never mind the fact that you are qualified, or that you have years of experience, or that you have hundreds of business contacts. None of that matters. What matters is making the right connections at the right time. The moon and the stars must all align.

And then guess what? You actually have to *interview* or sell yourself to get the business. And I thought interviewing for a full-time job was hard! Consultancy requires a series of on-going interviews that never end.

It is not that people don't want to hire you. It is just that it's complicated. Some have long-standing agreements with other consultants. Some engage with big agencies that have large staffs to help with their business. It's a David versus Goliath situation in many cases, the independent consultant versus the behemoth, established, well-funded agency.

As a new consultant, I have had to pound the pavement to find opportunities, which takes time—lots of it. Time to network, indentify opportunities, meet people and foster relationships.

It takes time to find the jobs and to see any money as a result. That doesn't happen by simply hanging up your shingle.

Is it still worth it? For me it is. As one of my friends says, "You have to fish while you eat." But I don't mind. I am confident that I am in the right spot, and the fish will start biting soon.

It's Not You; It's Me

Am I Dating or
Am I Job Hunting?

Job hunting is a lot like dating—lots of chance happenings and promising connections, followed by long dry spells. At least that's what I remember about dating.

I'll admit it, putting myself out there in a job search is hard. It's tiring. It can even be boring. And it's depressing when I don't get a response. All those post-date questions come back to haunt me: Did I say something dumb? Did I look OK? Was I wearing the right shoes?

There is a lot of down time between contacts—dry spells to ponder all those questions.

And suddenly ... *Ring! Ring!* Is that the phone? Careful not to answer on the first ring, lest I sound too anxious, I finally pick up. After all, I *did* learn something from my dating experiences.

It's a friend and former colleague with a job lead! Trying not to get too excited, I wonder if this could be "the one." Could this be Prince Charming, riding in on the white horse? I try not to notice the castle in the distance. Don't plan the wedding yet, I remind myself.

My friend gives me the name of the company and tells me to expect a call from the hiring manager on Monday. I'm leaving town for the weekend, so I take a few minutes to research the company online. Looks interesting; they do some sort of medical research, if I recall. I prepare a set of Q&A, my tool to help organize my answers to potential interview questions. I'm going to be ready, yessiree.

Now it's Monday. After a great weekend, I begin preparation for the call that will come in a few hours. Logging onto the computer, I Google the company to continue my research. Done, just as the phone rings!

Deep, cleansing breath—here we go. I'm picturing moving into the castle.

Things seem to be going well until the manager asks how I would handle a crisis plan for the company. I proceed to tell her my thoughts. Especially since their factory is in India, there could be a global crisis and we would need to consider many factors.

She stops me cold. "What on earth are you talking about," she says? I'm puzzled as I'm looking at the website and it lists the locations around the world. All of a sudden it clicks: I've researched the wrong company!

Aughhhhhh! And there goes prince charming ...

What happened, you ask? My friend and I never exchanged emails with the name of the company. She told me over the phone. When I typed in the company name from memory on the morning of my interview, I accidentally mistyped one letter. Ironically, the company that I researched—*the wrong company*—engages in almost exactly the same type of work as *the correct company*. What are the odds of two companies in the world doing very similar work with names that differ by only one letter?

At this point I just want the Earth to open and swallow me, or at least for the AT&T phone network to suddenly go down across the country. My face is ten shades of red, and I'm so glad we're not on Skype.

I apologize profusely, explaining what has happened. The hiring manager is not amused. Composing myself as best I can, we continue the interview. She says she will bring me in for another interview, only because I came highly recommended.

Then "click," and the phone is silent.

Any chance of living in that castle is history. Bye-bye, castle! Adios, Prince Charming!

Mortified, I immediately call my friend to explain what happened and offer my apologies—after all, it's her reputation on the line for recommending me. Luckily I have a very forgiving friend.

Unfortunately, the hiring manager is not so forgiving. I don't hear from her again.

Yep, this encounter will go down as the worst interview in history— at least in my history.

Someday this will be funny, right? I keep telling myself this over and over. If I ever overcome my embarrassment, I'll have a funny tale to share with my friends and colleagues. You are laughing, aren't you?

Did Etiquette Get Laid Off Too?

Excitement is in the air! An unsolicited call about a great opportunity has me riding high. A meeting is scheduled and I am ready to do this. Research is done; the company comes highly recommended. My wardrobe selection is made—it is important to look my best.

Show time! The meeting goes very well; the president and I seem to talk easily. Everyone is friendly. "You're great!" "No, you're great!" "Okay, we are all great!" The meeting of the mutual admiration society comes to a close.

"We will call you by the end of the week," they say. Wonderful! My handwritten thank-you notes go out that night. I'm really feeling good.

Friday comes and goes. No phone call. I send a quick email, reaffirming my interest in the company.

The next week begins, and before you know it another Friday is here. I double and triple check my phone to see if I have missed a call. How about my spam filter? Is there a message stuck in this black hole? Wait a second—I know what happened. They must have "lost" my phone number and email address. That has got to be it. I send another delightful note, declaring my interest in speaking with them again about the opportunity.

Two weeks later and not a peep. No call, no email, no Dear Jane letter, no smoke signals—nothing.

At this point, I'm just a teensy bit perturbed. Maybe a little hurt. Frustrated beyond belief.

Yoo-hoo! Hellooooo! Yes, you—the one at the desk on the top floor? Remember me?

The really sad thing is that this is not unusual. In speaking with my friends and colleagues, no response seems to be the norm.

You would think with multiple ways to contact people—phone, email, voicemail, text—that this would not be an issue. Maybe I should change my phone number to something more recognizable, like 867-5309? Then prospective employers could just sing my number ala Tommy Tutone—remember him from the '80s?

Whatever happened to common courtesy? Did etiquette get laid off too?

A simple call or email to say that, after careful consideration, you are going with a different candidate, that you've been busy, that you've been sick, that a herd of unicorns have held you hostage the last few weeks and you were unable to get to the phone? Anything would be better than nothing.

Knowledge is power, after all. My mantra as a boss and employee has always been that people can handle bad news—they just need to hear it. Not knowing the news is what's frustrating.

I get it—with hundreds or maybe thousands of applicants for a given position, combined with skeleton staffing, it is impossible to contact everyone who applies for a job.

However—*and this is big to those of us looking for work, so employers listen up*—it should be standard operating procedure to contact those applicants who actually landed an interview. Just a few words or a short email, informing the interviewee of the company's decision and providing the courtesy of an answer is the least that can be expected.

Not good at this? I'll write the script for you. It goes like this:
"Hello, Tami? This is Dave at XYZ company. Thank you so much for your interest in working here. We have had many great candidates, including you. I did want to let you know that we decided to move forward with another candidate. Thanks again for your interest. We wish you success in your job search." Click.

That wasn't so hard, was it? At most, you have spent five minutes on the phone providing the one thing candidates want after an interview: *an answer.* Even less time if you choose the email route. Hey, if you call at just the right moment, I won't be home and you can leave a message—no need to actually speak to me.

Kudos to the few companies out there that do actually follow-up with candidates. I wish there were more of you. In the meantime, those of us looking for our next opportunity are ready to hear from you. Good news or bad, we can handle it. We just want to get a call.

Dangling Carrots

I've said it before: job hunting is a lot like dating. For me, dating seems like such a long time ago. Yet I'm constantly reminded of it during my job search.

My strategy in dating was to cast a wide net in an attempt to find Mr. Right, or at least Mr. New Friend. It was hard work, networking with friends, accepting almost any invitation despite the long hours of prep work it required, including what to wear, gathering input from friends and working on strategy. Men have no idea how much time women spend selecting the right shoes to go with a date outfit.

I'd chuckle at all this planning, thinking, "It's just dinner, right?" One time I said as much to a dear friend who had accepted a date with a new guy, someone that none of us knew. As she came to me for advice, I boldly stated, "Go with him! It's just a movie; you're not marrying him." The joke was on all of us as I stood at their wedding a year later.

The "casting a wide net" part of my dating strategy eventually translated into my job search strategy. Just to be clear, I'm happily married and not looking for dates; we're just talking about jobs now. Hubby is breathing a sigh of relief.

Even when I was happily working full-time, I also had a job search strategy. That may seem odd to some, yet I think there's some validity to the saying, "It's easier to get a job when you have a job."

No matter how satisfied I was with my job, each year I challenged myself to get one job interview. By doing so, I was forced to keep my résumé up to date and also to examine my current situation lest I get complacent. I even had friends participate with me, and we held each other accountable.

Add a layoff to the equation and suddenly the search took on a more serious nature. The strategy became ... cast a wide net and accept meetings to discuss any reasonable opportunity that presents itself. Never hurts to talk right? My thinking has always been that "You can't turn it down until they make you an offer."

Or can you?

Shocking as this sounds, I'm beginning to think it's okay to turn down the offer, even if it is just to chat.

This is counterintuitive to those of us looking for our next opportunity. Shouldn't we knock ourselves out for each and every possible job lead?

It occurred to me some time ago—while I was casting my wide net—that accepting all opportunities to talk is not necessarily productive, especially when we know the opportunity is not right. Once I absorbed this "ah-ha" moment, I forced myself to stop, collect my thoughts, think long-term and develop a strategy. Starting with my end goal—the job I wanted—I worked my way back through the block and tackle tactics. I even developed a "wish list" for my ideal job, including corporate culture and commute. With this roadmap, I narrowed down the field of opportunities, but I also granted myself some freedom.

Freedom to decline opportunities that may sound great but ultimately steered me away from my goal. Freedom to work towards what I want to do for the next how-ever-many-years I'll be working.

Is this easy to do? Nope. It's hard to turn away unsolicited calls dangling the carrot of a potential job under our nose, especially those that, at any other time, would be a good fit. And it's flattering to hear someone show interest in us and our abilities. Kind of like dating, it's hard to turn something down for fear we may never have another date.

I'm okay with accepting offers to talk, if it's truly something of interest. But I can't let the dangling carrot steer me away from my goals.

Flattery:
The Ultimate Recruiting Tool

Today I received a call. Not just any call, mind you. This is the one I had been waiting for. Okay, I'm giving it more credit than it deserves. It was out-of-the-blue, totally unexpected, yet one that I was happy to get.

It was a call about a job opportunity. "We've reviewed your résumé and would like to talk to you about our firm, if you are still in the market for a new job."

Questions raced through my mind. I don't think I applied for this position, so how did she find me?

Yes, I tell her, I'm still "exploring opportunities." That's job-seeker code for "Thank goodness you called!" She tells me it's hard to believe someone of my caliber is available, that my qualifications are stellar and that, on paper at least, I'm just what they are looking for.

"Are you available to discuss?" Am I available? LOL! My calendar isn't exactly bursting with appointments right now, unless you count my laundry-folding meeting in the living room at 11:00, followed closely by a vacuuming seminar this afternoon. Not to mention the off-site at the grocery store, although I might be able to reschedule it.

She sends me information about the opportunity. I pore over her e-mail and look at the company's website all while taking notes. During our follow-up call, we discuss my background, details of the position and other general stuff.

"We'd like to bring you in for an interview with the hiring manager in a few days; we're on the fast-track to fill this position." And we're off! Amazing how quickly these things can happen. I'm a bit star-struck and over the moon. She thinks I'm perfect for the position. Her flattery is definitely nice to hear, especially having been in layoff land for a while.

Fast-forward a few days. Now that I know more about the position and have had time to digest the information, I have a nagging feeling—and not in a good way.

I push the feelings to the back of my mind, telling myself it's okay to talk to them. No harm in that, right? Just talk.

The more I think about the opportunity, the less interested I become. I find myself trying to see the positives, like "it's a good company" and "it would be a good resume builder," and my personal favorite, "at least it's a job." Hardly how I want to land my next gig.

Hubby comes home to find me sitting at my desk, pitch dark except for the glow of my computer screen. Immediately sensing that something is wrong, he tries to humor me and pull me out of my funk by turning on the lights. Poor decision on his part. I immediately snap at him and he wonders why, especially with the good news of a potential job.

"What's wrong?" he implores. "I thought they loved you."

And therein lays the problem. They do love me, my experience, my knowledge, etc. On paper, the job looks good in terms of commute and that it's in my industry. But that's where it stops. I'm not interested in the type of work they offer. It's sort of in my field, but at any other time I would not even consider this job.

Is it wrong to want to work at something you love? I don't think so. I learned a long time ago that while I can put on the occasional academy-award-winning performance when necessary, I'm not good when it comes to working at something I don't love. Some people can do just about anything in terms of work if the money and benefits are right. Not me. I have to be passionate about my work—to really feel it, loving what I do.

This reminds me of dating, although it's been awhile since I had to go through that sort of interviewing. Kind of like the cute guy you've been secretly eyeing, hoping he would call for a date. When he finally calls, it's all hearts and flowers and puppy dogs and everything else wonderful you can imagine. Until you actually have a one-on-one date and realize that while he may be easy on the eyes, he can't hold a conversation unless it's about his model pony collection.

I must admit the recruiter had me at "we love your experience." It's unbelievably flattering to have someone want me for a job, even if it's not the best fit. And it's hard to separate the flattery from the realization that, while it may be a good job opportunity, it's just not the right one.

My decision? Difficult as it was, I took the bold step to thank them profusely for considering me and politely declined.

If loving my career is wrong, I don't wanna be right.

Debit or Credit?

Vegetables:
Are They Really a Necessity?

I woke up with a fever. Something I've dreaded since winter began. I could feel it all over, to my very core. I'm not sure I can handle this right now.

Is it the flu? Pneumonia? Some new virus brought on by the mosquitoes that have already started feeding on me in this balmy March weather?

No, this one is far more dangerous, especially to our checkbook.

I have shopping fever.

Those of you who don't like to shop may not understand this, or will for sure underestimate the torture of this insidious ailment. It feels like every store in the mall is calling me. Nordstrom says, "Our shoes are on sale." Ann Taylor's teasing me with her, "Buy any two items, get 20% off" deal. And don't get me started on what the handbag stores are saying. New styles at Vuitton, Coach, Dooney & Bourke—catch me before I faint!

I can hear them pleading with me to visit, "Just take a look. We haven't seen you in quite some time," they say. "See all the new fashions; the 'must-haves' for spring that are perfect for you. It won't hurt just to look, will it?"

"No!" I say out loud as I try with all my might to steer my car away from that mall Mecca we in Dallas call NorthPark Centre. MUST-RESIST-TEMPTATION. How will I ever get through this?

I divert my attention to our local Sam's, hoping to satisfy my shopping fever by taking care of the necessities, like groceries. As I bravely march up and down the food aisles, my fever rises again and I veer off to the other side of the store. How about a 55" TV? That would be nice. Surely we could use a 12-pack of reading glasses. No, wait—how about a complete set of wrenches?

What does shopping have to do with being laid off? *EVERYTHING*.

One of the by-products of losing your job is worry—especially about money. How to pay the mortgage, expenses such as the car, kids' college, any debt you might have. Hubby and I have been in this state for almost two years. He won the layoff bingo first; I followed a year later.

Try as we might to not dwell on money, it seeps into almost everything we do. We were used to a very comfortable income with both of us employed, one that allowed us to rarely question the periodic need to shop. New shoes? Sure. Another suit? Why not? Besides, you *need* it for work.

Since the layoffs, we question every purchase, even at the grocery store. We debate whether we really need "designer" lettuce or will iceberg do? How about colas? We shouldn't drink those anyway.

Deodorant? I really don't think anyone will get close enough to smell us. And what about vegetables? They're pricey. Are they really necessary?

I'm only half-kidding. For us, the decision to devise a layoff financial plan was a no-brainer. We approached this new phase of our lives like we were going into battle. Operation "self-imposed poverty" was our strategy. No cable, no concerts, no shopping for clothes, more eating at home—all in the plan.

We count our blessings daily. Thank goodness for our parents, who instilled in us the need to always save, no matter how much you make. *Dad, I wish you were here to see that I listened and learned from you.* We both have found ways to bring in money, enough that it's like we are living on one of our salaries. And that works.

Do I still have "shopping fever"? You betcha. Yet I know that this too shall pass. My "need" for shoes is really just a "want."

Although watch out, mall. When I get back to work, I'm coming to visit. I may even buy something.

Mail Call

We have a ritual in our house when it comes to mail. Mail is brought in and divided into three categories: junk mail, bills and magazines/catalogues. It is an easy task to rifle through the stack of mail and toss the obvious junk items. "No, for the umpteenth time we do not need a coupon for a new air conditioner—we used your coupon last year when we had to replace our old one. Don't you guys check your mailing lists?"

We sometimes fight over who goes to the mailbox because the fun part is that whoever gets the mail gets dibs on looking through the stack for the good stuff. Usually meaning, he or she gets the first look at the new *People* magazine. It's definitely important to be the first in the family to know just how the Kardashians are faring in this economy.

The remaining mail—the bills—begins a tour of the house. At first they land on the kitchen counter, then they spend some time on the table. Sometimes they get to see the couch. At some point in the next, oh, week or so, they move to the desk near the computer, ready to be paid. Unfortunately we tend to forget about them.

When both of us worked full-time, sixty-hour-a-week jobs, bill paying was done quickly as a team. When Hubby was laid off, he took over bill paying on a regular basis. Sweet! I was off the hook.

Then our roles reversed and the honor of bill paying was bestowed on me. Not my favorite task, but I'll do it. It makes me nervous, watching the money exit our account like water through a sieve, with only one paycheck coming in where there used to be two.

On a positive note, it does force me to examine our finances. We have always been good at budgeting and saving so I suppose I should be happy that we are not overextended. We are actually in good shape. But I'm still sad. For both the loss of one income and the loss of the money we could have saved with that extra income.

Who am I kidding? I am really sad about the lack of new shoes in my closet. Have you seen my new shoes? Neither have I—*there aren't any!*

Here's what bugs me the most: we are comfortably living on one income when we used to have two. How can that be? What did we do with the money from the second paycheck? I didn't buy *that* many pairs of shoes.

Let's see where the extra moolah went …

Housekeeping
We used to have our house cleaned every other week. Now we are down to once a month. A luxury yes, but the only way to maintain harmony in the house since Hubby and I have diametrically opposed cleaning styles. To say he is meticulous is an understatement. I will have vacuumed, dusted and straightened the entire house and he is still cleaning one shower. We don't have to eat there, just shower.

Cable

Okay, no savings there. We have never had cable or satellite. Yes, I know—we are the only people anywhere without this luxury. At least that is what our nieces and nephews tell us.

Travel

Fun weekend trips used to always be a part of our routine before the layoff. Nowadays we stay closer to home, although we do still manage to drive out to far North Dallas on occasion. Sometimes we will venture as far as Frisco. Whew, now that's a trip—we have to pack a lunch. You can almost see the Oklahoma border, if you look close enough.

Shoes and Clothing

Savings here, for sure. Definitely not much new in either of our closets. Nordstrom probably wonders what happened to us.

Doggie Day Care

Gone—even the dog had to make a sacrifice. Besides she is no longer a puppy with tons of energy. She spent much of her daycare time just laying around watching the other dogs in action.

Eating Out

We have definitely cut back on this. Our sincerest apologies to our favorite Mexican restaurant; we are sure they had to layoff a waiter or two due to our absence.

Entertainment

Why pay for entertainment when free stuff reigns? There are tons of festivals and free or low-cost events around town. We have not been to a concert in ages; we actually think our hearing has improved since we are not subjected to such high decibel levels. Haven't been to the movie theater much either. Last weekend was our first movie in a long time, and it was such a treat to have a date. Well, I'm not sure this classified as a real date. The movie was at 10:00 am to take advantage of the early-bird ticket price, hardly a date-like ambiance. But hey, we were out.

Looking at this list makes me even more depressed. Not for the things we are missing, but for the realization that with a few living adjustments, we easily could have saved one entire salary.

We have definitely learned a thing or two from the layoffs, especially the way we think about money. It has actually been very freeing, knowing that not only can we survive on one salary, but we can live comfortably doing it.

Of course, I still yearn for new shoes.

Financing a Layoff

When I was a kid, I always looked forward to Saturdays. On Saturdays I got to sleep late. More importantly, Saturday was "allowance day." Dad would go to his dresser and ceremoniously bestow my weekly allowance. My insides would tingle as he placed the money in my hands. It was definitely the highlight of my week.

Immediately upon receiving the cash, Dad's voice would turn more gravelly and ominous than usual as he told me, "Be sure to pay yourself first."

Sweet! I would have been happy to pay myself in candy or movie tickets or some other treat. Unfortunately, that's not what Dad meant.

I had to take half my allowance and put it in my piggy bank. *I had to save it*. Dreams of a movie or candy shopping trip would come to a screeching halt.

To give you a better understanding of my disappointment, let's talk about how much allowance I got each week that would make me cringe at putting some in the bank. Are you ready? *Fifty cents*. Two quarters each week. One for me and one for Miss Piggy Bank.

At this rate I was never going to become the next Trump or Buffett or even come close to making Forbes' richest list.

I'd ask why—"Why, Dad, do I have to save this money?" He'd always say it was for college. Okay, that sounded reasonable. I was sure college was going to ROCK because I'd have all the money from my bank to play with.

Similar thing happened at Christmas. Each year I received money from several great aunts and great uncles, most of whom I had never met. They were quite generous, these relatives/strangers. As soon as I would open the card with the money, Dad would take the money to put into my savings account. Again with the statement, "It's for college."

I began to hate Miss Piggy Bank, plotting her demise every time I was denied a purchase because I didn't have enough money.

Fast-forward to college. "Dad, can I use the money in Miss Piggy Bank?" Nope. That money is for when you start your career.

Huh? What the? I'm going to make tons of money, Dad. Surely Miss Piggy Bank can spare a starving student a dime?

At graduation I almost didn't ask, but of course I had to. "Dad, is it time to use the money? I need to buy a car." "No," he said, "That money is for your wedding."

Didn't matter that I was not even close to the altar. That money stayed put, and kept coming in. Those generous relatives/strangers sent money each year from the time I was an infant until they passed away when I was an adult with a career. And each time I spoke to Dad he'd ask about my job, and if I was "paying myself first." "Uh, yeah, Dad, I'm saving some money." Didn't have the heart to tell him I didn't save half of my salary.

As my career progressed and my salary increased, Dad made sure I knew the benefits of a 401K, in addition to "paying myself first." As a single gal, I never felt quite comfortable with my financial security and decided that saving was a good way to protect myself just in case I lost my job.

The savings really ramped up when I met Hubby. He had been brought up in a similar manner, being forced to budget and save. Together, we set financial goals and figured out how to meet them. Even though we were quite comfortable with our double-income lifestyle, we constantly saved, doing without things like cable and the latest gadget. We also began our "ten-year car plan," which meant driving our cars for at least ten years in an effort to have only one car payment at any given time.

Just to be clear, we have never felt deprived. We have just always chosen very carefully how to spend our money.

Then the layoffs hit, first Hubby and then me. We panicked momentarily the day of Hubby's layoff, as we had never been without two incomes. That very night we began a new financial strategy called "operation self-imposed poverty." Hubby quickly found a few part-time jobs and landed full-time contract work before it was my turn to be laid off.

I have thought a lot about Dad during this layoff period—Dad and his "pay yourself first" mentality. Never did I think that the philosophy he shared with me would make a big difference, yet I realize now the lesson he was teaching: to save something from each paycheck, each financial windfall. It's okay to spend some, but you have to save. Always.

I used to wonder why Dad gave me two quarters, making me put one in Miss Piggy Bank. He could easily have done that himself and just given me one quarter. Ah, but that was the lesson. I had to physically and mentally learn to take my money and put it into savings.

Thank goodness I paid attention to Dad's foolishness. By "paying ourselves first," we have been relatively comfortable during our layoffs. And guess what? Because saving was ingrained in my psyche, we have continued to save even in unemployment.

All because of two quarters a week, and a Dad who insisted that I learn the lesson.

Am I Allowed a Spring Break?

It's spring break! I just found out. How exciting!

And how did I know that it's spring break time? My nieces and nephews? Friends with kids? Neighboring families asking to take in their mail while they're gone?

Nope. I found out from adult friends, those whose kids are way beyond school age, some of these friends are beyond retirement age, even. They are the ones going on spring break trips.

Say what?

Since when did this school-era right to a vacation become a hit with the over 40 crowd? And more importantly, why weren't my husband and I informed of this trend? Clearly we are out of the loop when it comes to spring break.

The trips these folks are taking are right up there with the college-aged crowd. A neighbor in his 70s is going skiing. Another couple is headed to the beach in Costa Rica. Others are going to Vegas. Sure hope I don't see anyone I know in a "Girls Gone Wild" or "MTV Spring Break" episode.

I would love to be on a beach right now—all sunshine, blue skies and warm temperatures. Maybe we should go on spring break too. I can picture myself on the beach, by a pool, on the slopes— anywhere but here, in front of the computer.

Never has a vacation been needed as much as it is now, at least for us. I never realized how tiring and emotionally draining it is to exist in "career transition." Yet I feel funny even considering a vacation. After all, I'm not really working. I'm just looking for a job.

In my line of thinking, no work means no need for vacation. *Right?*

The idea of a vacation during this time is really scary. I've been conditioned to spend all my time looking for my next opportunity. What if I miss a great opportunity because I'm on vacation? What if I spend some money? Shouldn't that be kept for emergencies? What if, what if, what if?

What if I forgot, even for short time, that I was looking for a job?

Just like when I was working, I need a break from my weekly routine. While my current work issues are different than when I sat at my office job, it's stressful just the same. Almost more stressful. And just because I'm not working doesn't mean that I shouldn't take a break.

So maybe I'll take a week for spring break too. Maybe we can declare a truce with our electronic devices, no looking at job boards or networking, at least for a few hours each day.

No, we aren't jetting off to a tropical locale. But sitting in my backyard with a good book sure is looking good.

Home Sweet Home Office

Woof! My Executive Assistant is Calling

Working from home—isn't that the dream of anyone who sits in an office, or even worse, cubicle-land? To be free to work when we want, dressed in our jammies and slippers, with a commute that amounts to about 15 steps? Ah … the life!

Working from home has always been my dream. I envied the consultants who worked for me, coming to my office only for critical meetings and the occasional lunch.

In thinking about my new venture as a consultant, the positives seem obvious. *Need to be home to meet the plumber?* No prob! *Beautiful day outside?* Take the laptop and work on the patio. Grocery shop when there's no crowd; work in the evening. Hit the gym while taking a break from the desk. *Wow, this will be great.*

The best of both worlds … working while enjoying my home.

What I didn't count on are the many distractions that accompany an at-home office.

As I'm thinking about a strategy document, my mind wanders. What kind of shelving unit should we purchase for the home office? This leads to measuring the available space against the wall. *Must get back to work.* Sitting down; doing well so far. Out of the corner of my eye I see the laundry room. What a great opportunity to run a load of clothes! After all, I'm working from home. Machine purrs with the laundry running. *Back at the desk again.* Oops, bathroom break; should have done that while I was working on the laundry. Passing the kitchen back to the office, I see coffee—that would taste good. Coffee in hand, I'm back at the desk reviewing the two lines I've completed since my 9 am start. Ring! The phone—no, I don't want to contribute to your campaign, or take a magazine subscription, or whatever it is you want. *Whew. Finally back to work.* Ding Dong! Oh yeah, I did schedule an A/C service. Weren't you supposed to be here at 8am? Cool air on now, *sitting down again at my desk to work.*

Noon already? I have a call with a client. Just as we are getting into the heart of our discussion, I hear "Woof!" My 80-lb dog sees something in the backyard and wants out. I put my fingers to my lips to shush her, like she really knows what that means. Again, *Woof, Woof, Woof* … she is growing louder with each bark. I try to stay focused on the call, listening and taking notes. My dog is pacing the living room in circles, running in to my office to make sure I heard her, looking at me, pleading with her eyes. Woof! Woof! Grrr … Woof! *Danger, Mom! It's a Code Red in the backyard!* Clearly she thinks the neighborhood squirrels are launching an attack, and it's her job to get out there.

Exasperated, frustrated, embarrassed, I have to break away from my client to let the dog out. "Excuse me, but my executive assistant is barking."

Back on the call ... where were we? Oh yes—the plan for this spring. Here we go ... *scratch, scratch*. Yes we were talking about marketing ... *scratch, rattle, scratch*. What the heck is that? The dog—my protector, my pal—is scratching at the door, insisting that she come inside immediately. Danger is over in the yard. Trying not to disrupt the call again, I quietly switch to speakerphone and tiptoe to the door to let her in.

What was that you said? My apologies, this phone is not too good. *Apparently, I stepped out of hearing range to get the dog.*

So this is what it's like to work at home? An endless series of interruptions, from my wandering mind, the dog, the phone? I thought this would be much easier.

Six o'clock—Hubby, you're home so soon! But I'm not finished working; where did the day go? Yes, dinner, walking the dog, and the gym ... let's go.

Woof! Woof! You're right, my trusty—yet distracting—executive assistant. I can finish working later. I get to work from home.

Is My Underwear Showing?

I love looking at interior design magazines, especially those that feature ultra-contemporary homes. So crisp and clean, everything is pristine and no clutter in sight. Friends could appear at these homes at any time, day or night, and the place would look the same. Perfectly organized.

I hate the people who live in these homes. And I don't even know them.

One of my dreams is to be so completely organized that I too could have friends drop in unannounced without worrying about our clean underwear that managed to make it from the dryer to the living room couch, but never folded itself and got to the chest of drawers in the bedroom.

Despite the possible underwear sighting, our clutter is usually under control. Until you get to the home office.

At previous jobs, many times I would walk by a co-worker's desk and stare with envy: color-coordinated folders neatly organized in a file holder, a container with just the right amount of pens, a clutter-free desk that screams "put something on me, please!" And everything uniformly coded with labels from an over-used Brother P-Touch.

My desk, on the other hand, always looked like a cross between an organization project in progress and a junk pile. My inbox (a concept I have always hated) was more of a receptacle for "things I'll read later." My administrative assistants have always known better than to put anything of importance in that black hole. If you want me to see it, put it on my chair so I can sit on it. When I am uncomfortable enough, I will pull it out from under me and look at it. Seriously, I used to do this.

Multiple cups of pens and pencils, a business card holder, a couple of notebooks, sticky notes and umpteen folders in assorted stacks have always made up my work areas. A blanket is always draped haphazardly on the back of my chair so I'm ready when the arctic blast of the A/C comes on. An assortment of trinkets has always shared the shelf space with awards and books. My "filing" has always been on my desk. If a folder actually made it to the file drawer, I would "lose" it, unable to figure out where I put it.

And then there was my "drink buffet," as friends affectionately called it. Always present was a big glass of water, a coffee mug and sometimes a soft drink. Never hurts to be hydrated.

I have never found time to be as organized as the photos in the magazines or some of the desks that I envied. I always thought that if I worked from home, things would be different. The interior design magazines would all be calling, wanting to capture my fabulous home office in pictures for all to see.

Yeah, right. I believe my home office might even be worse than the ones I had at work. Sigh.

So what if my home office is not exactly a shining example of organization skills? As long as it works for me, right? I've been trying to relax and not worry about keeping a tidy desk.

Then I read an article that implied a person's professionalism may be at risk if her workspace is cluttered. Hmm …

Some of the points in the article:

- Keep only materials you need for current projects on your desk. *Okay, I need everything. If I didn't need it, I'd throw it away. Duh.*

- Don't pile papers; put them in designated areas or give them to your colleagues. *Where's my designated colleague? The one that's supposed to take care of my papers? Is this article for real? Guess I didn't negotiate a "D.C." into my self- employment agreement.*

- Go paperless, printing only when necessary. *This may be okay if you don't get many emails with attachments, but with an inbox hitting 3,000 it is better to print than to try and find what you need at a moment's notice.*

- Don't touch the same piece of paper twice. *Huh? How do they ever get any work done? I'm sorry, I would love to re-read your memo, but I can't touch the paper again.*

You know what I think? A cluttered desk might be a good thing, the sign of someone who is incredibly busy getting work done. I think that those who have a completely clean desk may not have enough work to do. Yep, if they were busy, they would not have time to wear out their Brother P-Touch. They would be multi-tasking from one project to the next, jumping from one messy pile of folders to the other while conducting a conference call with 40 people at the same time.

One thing I know for sure: I can put my hand on any folder I might need from the stacks on my desk, even if I were blindfolded.

Interior design magazines, you may still come by and see my office, complete with coffee mugs and piles of folders. Just ignore the underwear in the living room.

I Love You. Now
Please Leave Me Alone

One of the best times in my life was when now-Hubby asked me to marry him. I was over the moon! He was (and still is) my prince, and the opportunity to spend the rest of my life with him was irresistible. Yep, he had me at "hello." After spending years as a single gal focused on the three C's (career, clothing, car), I was ready to settle down and make a new life together.

Of course when I said "yes," it never occurred to me exactly how this would affect my day-to-day life. Take living arrangements, for example. I was one of those people who really enjoyed living alone. I loved having my own space, and after great times with friends I could always escape to my apartment for some "me time."

Odd as this may seem, I used to relish the occasional Saturday night alone. I would take myself out to dinner and pick up an early edition of the Sunday paper. At home I would spread the paper out and read every page while listening to a TV show in the background. "Me time" at its best.

A couple of weeks before the wedding, I was hit with the revelation that I would have to share my sanctuary when Hubby moved in. In a moment of boldness, which Hubby instantly regretted, he had the nerve to ask if he could move his "stuff" in the week before the wedding so he would not have to pay another month's rent on his bachelor pad. Made perfect sense … to him.

I, on the other hand, saw this as an invasion and realized my "alone" time was about to change forever. My head may have actually twisted a full 360 degrees as I said—no, shrieked—something to the effect of, "Why do you have to live here? Can't you rent the apartment next door?"

Amazingly, Hubby didn't leave me on the spot.

After breathing into a paper bag for several hours (okay, days), I came around. This prince of a guy was more important than me having personal space and closet space. *Sort of.* I negotiated him down to using the unlit coat closet in the hall for his stuff, and his dresser had to live in another room. But he was in.

Fast forward 15 years, and I can't imagine life without Hubby. He is simply the best. Although most of his "stuff" never made it in the house, except for his clothes and dresser. Funny how that happened.

Yet I still crave alone time, whether it's finding time to pursue personal goals or simply having time to myself. To say it is a big challenge is an understatement. It's a constant struggle to balance work/home/family/me. You would think this would be relatively easy without human kids. *Yes Kylie, you are my wonderful four-legged daughter, but I can leave you alone in the house for a while as long as you have fresh water. Last time I checked this was not appropriate for children.*

With the layoffs came another layer of complexity. Both of us have worked at several things as we carve out the "new normal" in our lives. Juggling multiple pursuits saps all our energy and has severely cut into any "me time" I once had. I am torn too, because I would like to be with Hubby during the little bit of free time that we do have.

Hats off to those of you who successfully work from home. I am not sure how you do it. I originally thought that working out of the home office would be the perfect scenario. I was a teensy bit wrong on that one. No, I was horribly wrong. I am unable to separate my work environment from my home, always feeling the need to be in the office working on something. Instead of being easy and convenient, I have become a slave to my desk and computer. None of this is good for finding "me time."

So what's a girl to do? I certainly don't have the answer to this dilemma. I keep wishing things would go back to normal, the way they were before the layoffs, when we were just two crazy kids each working 60 hours a week.

I am going to keep looking for ways to get "me time." Until then, Hubby I adore you, I love you, now please leave me alone.

Making Lemonade

Vikings and Margaritas

Each summer, back when I was single, our group of friends would hold a "Viking Funeral Party." This consisted of a margarita machine, tons of food, music and as many friends as the house and yard could hold. Yes, I'm positive Vikings were fond of margaritas. Or they would have been, if they knew about them.

The main event of the Viking Funeral Party came late in the evening. A plastic wading pool filled with water was the focal point of the yard. A "boat" had been painstakingly hand-crafted specifically for this event.

In case you are unaware, legend has it that when Vikings died their bodies were placed on a floating vessel, along with their possessions. The vessel was then torched and pushed out into open water. Good-bye, Viking! At least this is my understanding of it.

Our version? We used this party as an opportunity to "put out to sea" something bad that had happened to us. It could be something humorous or very serious.

When all were assembled in the yard, each of us would tell the group what we were burning/getting rid of/forgetting, and place the item or a representation of the item on the boat. One guy burned a "Dear John" letter from an old flame. I burned my hospital bill from a devastating surgery. A dear friend burned a skimpy undergarment, saying "What was I thinking when I bought this?" All in good fun, we then set the boat on fire as the stereo blasted "Disco Inferno" as loud as possible.

I'm surprised the neighbors never complained, what with the toxic fumes from our boat. Yuck. Never did learn to build a good boat.

This memory got me thinking: could losing your job be a good reason to throw a party?

Maybe it's the best time to throw a party. Say goodbye to the past and look forward to a bright future. At the very least, it's an opportunity to put some closure to a life-changing event.

Honestly, our jobs weren't perfect were they? Sure, there were benefits—income, friends, mostly enjoyable work, possibly free coffee and, if you were lucky, a cubicle with a view. If you were fortunate enough to have a real office with a door, then you were among the extremely lucky.

No matter how much we enjoyed our jobs, there were negatives as well. Think about it for a minute; it wasn't all roses.

Unless you live next door, there's the commute through traffic. And long hours—fifty-plus hour workweeks were the norm for me. Small staffs. Limited funding. Frustration. Trying to make something from nothing. It's hard to keep going when you're asked to build Trump Tower on a Log Cabin budget.

Should we rejoice that we don't have jobs? Not really. I'm merely suggesting that we take the opportunity to cast the negative feelings from a job loss out to sea and start carving out a new future. It may not be the same as what we had in the past, but it can be equally as good—maybe even better.

I'll put my pink slip and COBRA info on the boat this year. Burn, Baby Burn, Disco Inferno! I feel better already. Everything's going to be great.

Expecting the Unexpected

I don't remember my first vacation—probably because I was six months old. Mom took me to see grandma, traveling on a combination of planes and trains. No wonder I like to travel and prefer faster transportation than driving.

Since we always lived far away, visits to relatives meant flying, which was very exciting as a child, and always included a new outfit to wear to give a great first impression as we deplaned. Sis and I each had our own carry-on that Mom packed with an assortment of new books, crayons, paper and whatever else might keep us entertained. She also traveled with snacks, despite the fact that Sis and I always looked forward to the airplane meal.

Mom was prepared, knowing that travels do not always go as planned. Glad I experienced this learning as a kid, since I've had my share of travel "adventures."

Take our honeymoon. Hubby took great pride in planning our trip to Rome. Happy but exhausted from the flight, we arrived at the hotel. "Don't worry about this room; it's for tonight only," said the front desk manager. Hmmm. We followed the bellman into the mini-elevator built for two, exited several floors later, then down the hall and around the corner to a red velvet curtain. As the bellman pulled the curtain back, we noticed the sign "Uscita Fuoco"—Fire Exit. With a grand gesture he opened the door, wedging it with a rock lest it slam shut and urged us to follow him.

Up the stone steps to the first landing we followed. Wait a second—are we on the fire escape? He pulled out a skeleton key—no, I'm not kidding—and opened a door, where we entered what appeared to be someone's apartment. And not a very nice one either. "Tomorrow, you change rooms," and he left. Ciao to you too, pal.

Not exactly how we planned to start our honeymoon. The only way to get back into the hotel was to walk five flights down the fire escape to the only door that would open from the outside, leading us straight into the manager's office. At least we had his attention.

Today this is a funny story. Hubby will confirm that this was not funny at the time. Exhausted, with nerves on end, I did what any good bride would have done in the same situation: I bawled—big tears, quivering lips, the whole works. Husband test number one: console new wife in fire escape room. After I calmed down, we decided to roll with it, venturing out to explore and have dinner. The next day we got to choose our "permanent room," ending up with a lovely room overlooking the piazza.

When my college roommate and I went to Australia, we tried to find something familiar for dinner so we ordered prawns—shrimp to us Texans. We knew a good meal and some sleep would power us through the jetlag. When the waiter brought us our meals, we just stared. And the prawns stared back at us. You see, they were artfully arranged as though they were dancing on the dish, their heads, tentacles, feet, hands, ears, noses and all other body parts intact. I think our blank stares told the waiter that we had no idea what to do with this dish, and he nicely took it to the kitchen to make it more user-friendly.

Hubby and I recently spent a few days in Paris. Venturing into the neighborhood around our hotel, it didn't match our expectations of "Gay Paree." We figured out the subway and made our way to the Seine, the Eiffel Tower and the Arch d' Triumph. Paris as we envisioned!

It wasn't until the second night that we realized where we were. Just down the block from our hotel, we noticed lots of neon signs and people outside, smiling at us as we passed by. When we saw the merchandise in the stores with the big neon signs, it dawned on us. We were in the red light district! No wonder everyone was so friendly.

Yep, traveling—especially abroad—is full of unexpected happenings. Usually there are only two things you can do in these situations: make the best of it or have a meltdown. Hubby and I choose to expect the unexpected and make the best of it, adapting to each situation as we go—after my meltdown of course.

Unemployment is usually unexpected. Although now it is something we should all prepare for, because at some point it will probably happen to each of us. We can't stop layoffs from happening, but we can save money, network like crazy, learn new skills and keep our eyes open for new opportunities—even if we are employed. The best time to prepare for the unexpected is when things are stable.

Hubby and I plan to return to Paris someday to see more of the city. We will ride the subways again and go to the Eiffel Tower. We may even visit the red light district. But we will plan to stay elsewhere.

The Cavalry Isn't Coming

The phone calls and emails are amazing. Friends and family all touching base with me, to make sure I'm okay. Let's meet for coffee! Let's go to lunch! I'll bring you a meal! Okay, that last one's an exaggeration. But everyone has good intentions to support me through the world of unemployment and job search.

At first, it's like a great flood. My calendar was booked with all sorts of Starbucks get-togethers and networking lunches. I never knew I had so many friends. What a great person I must be!

Then, just like tabloid news, it gets old. The calls become few and far between. Suddenly, it's radio silence.

Hello? Is anybody out there? I still like coffee and am available for lunch. Anyone?

Has everyone abandoned me? Of course not! I have one of the best support networks anywhere. The reality is my friends have very busy lives already, just like I did when I was when juggling a full-time job and home life. Most importantly, I'm responsible for my job search and social calendar, not them.

And the last time I checked, social networks go two ways. I could contact people as well, ya know.

Yet in my attempt to find meaning in this world of unemployment, the computer has become like a drug, making me cocoon inside the office, creating ways to stay busy. I've become addicted to staring at the screen, staring into nothingness. The more I stay home in front of the computer the more reclusive I become—very odd for an outgoing social butterfly like me.

What to do, what to do. How do I get out of this rut?

Several options come to mind:

- Set up a welcome table at Starbucks to recruit new friends. *Seems sort of stalkerish to me.*

- Become a mall walker. All day. Every day. *Also high in the creepy factor, especially for store employees who would see me daily.*

- Fix the backyard fence. *Seems like that might be tough on my nails—no pun intended.*

- Work in the yard. *Um ... that's just not gonna happen.*

- Become a world champion computer solitaire player. *Is there money in this?*

Or how about a completely passive approach? Surely if I sit here long enough the phone will ring. After all, I'm completely up to speed on the latest celebrity gossip from reading *People*. That's got to be of value to someone.

After much thought and too many Mrs. Field's cookies (the mall walking thing was not a good idea), I come up with the only truly viable option: use my MBA mind to develop a business strategy that will pave the way to my next opportunity. *Just like I would do in any corporate business situation.*

As a dear friend once told me, "The cavalry isn't coming."

Are you sure, I ask him? I look out the window. After all, what if they are just down the street?

Of course they're not coming, even here in Texas, where cowboys and boots and horses are common.

The cavalry is actually waiting for *me* to call *them*. I have to get out and make my own destiny. Seize each and every opportunity to network, follow up on leads, improve my skills by taking classes— in other words, apply my hard-earned knowledge, do the work and find the next opportunity myself.

Many people I know have succumbed to idleness, waiting for opportunity to ring the doorbell, send a text, friend them on Facebook, Tweet them a new job. In fact, these people have become masters at waiting. It is a routine that is easy to fall into when we don't have a job to go to. The hardest part is to keep the momentum going and resist lapsing into laziness.

I believe most of us in the job hunt want to find work and be productive, yet our approach lacks a strategy. Yes, occasionally a recruiter will call out of the blue, but isn't it better to be productive? Waiting for the phone is about as motivating as watching paint dry.

This is not good news for some folks. They want the next job handed to them on a silver platter. Oh boy, have I got news for them.

What is that, you say? You think I'm being too harsh? My point is that we—you and I—need to take responsibility for our situation and go on the attack. Be aggressive in our job searches. Develop a strategy. Plan the work and work the plan. Network like there's no tomorrow. Keep putting one foot in front of the other. Never give up. The cavalry's out there to help us; we just have to send them a signal.

I've got my cowboy boots on and am ready to go. Are you?

Winner, Winner, Chicken Dinner!

The reception is the best part about a wedding, isn't it? Unless you're the bride or groom, of course. They're busy being serious, taking vows. The rest of us in attendance are getting serious about the party after the ceremony. Food plus drinks plus dancing equals fun!

Recently, I had the opportunity to attend a wedding reception—a beautiful affair at the top of one of the tallest buildings in town, with a panoramic view of the city. The room was fully decorated, flowers, bartenders and wait staff; even the chairs were dressed in fine linens for the occasion. And of course there were the traditional cakes: vanilla for the bride, and chocolate for the groom. Honestly, I don't know why we even bother with vanilla when we all really want chocolate, but that's another story.

Yet this was an odd wedding reception because there was no wedding.

Apparently the groom backed out a few weeks in advance—enough time to warn the bride, yet not enough time to recoup the money for the reception. The bride and her family decided to make lemonade out of the giant lemon they were holding, giving the reception to two nonprofits for their use. Talk about class!

I was invited to speak at the soiree by friends who were using this good fortune to launch their new nonprofit. The huge party space had been divided into two, with one nonprofit on each side of the room. A small dance floor was the only separation. Sort of like we did when we were kids on a road trip when we drew a line down the center of the backseat, with each of us taking a side.

Both events took place at the same time, with each group trying to focus their attention on their own presentation. The humorous part is that the wait staff treated both events as one big party.

As I was speaking to our group, out of the corner of my eye I could see the other group mingling at the bar, which happened to be on their side of the room. Lucky dogs. I sat down, and another speaker began. As if on cue, the entire wait staff descended with trays bearing flutes of champagne. Obviously we were supposed to toast the "bride." From my seat, I could see the other side of the room trying to decide what to do with their champagne as well. Calm heads prevailed as we collectively made the decision that good champagne should not go to waste.

Our speaker finished, and we were ready to eat. Ah ... but the other group's presentation was still in progress. Guess we have to wait for dinner. BUT NO! The wait staff suddenly appeared with salads, during the middle of their presentation. At that point, we all realized that our party was their party, and vice versa.

Sensing our hunger, or possibly hearing our stomachs growling, the wait staff served our side first. Winner, winner, chicken dinner!

Why do they always serve chicken at these things?

Our table had been joking about dessert actually being wedding cake. We really didn't *expect* wedding cake. Until we saw the saber-wielding wait person arrive with a cart full of plates. It really was a wedding reception ... without the bride and groom. But why wedding cake? The caterer had three weeks' notice. Did they really make the cakes that far in advance?

As we all enjoyed cake and pondered the generosity of the bride and her family, a more important thought crossed my mind.

Getting jilted by the one you love is a devastating blow. Picking yourself up afterwards and moving on with your life has got to be tough. Not to mention what do you do with the dress? It's not like you can turn all that satin and lace into a nifty little sundress to wear at the pool. Heaven forbid you have dyed-to-match shoes. Try walking in them out to the pool.

Yet isn't this situation eerily similar to being laid off? Getting jilted by your employer, especially if you liked your job, can be devastating. The thought of losing your job, your friends, your stability, your income, your sense of self can be heartbreaking. Just like the jilted bride, those who lose their jobs can find themselves feeling alone on an island—without a ticket to go home.

Despite the trauma, the most important thing we can do when we lose our job is to stand up, brush ourselves off, hold our heads up, and move on. Have a party if you want, something to start a new chapter in your life. *Just keep moving forward.*

I would like to thank the bride and her family for the wonderful party. It was lovely, and our new nonprofit definitely appreciated the generosity.

Next time—if there is a next time—just serve chocolate cake. It's what we all want.

Fear of Flying

In general, there seems to be a growing fear when it comes to air travel. Maybe it has been this way for a while, and I am just now taking notice. As a frequent traveler myself, I think this fear is a bit silly. But to those caught in its grips, this fear is very, very real.

Many of you know what I am talking about, although you may not admit it. It begins at home as you are packing; the fear increasing in intensity as you near the airport. Once at the terminal, your palms become sweaty, grip tightening as you desperately try to avoid eye contact with airline employees.

"Hello! Welcome to our airline. May I see your identification?" Whew, you think to yourself—dodged that!

Once through security you feel a bit more at ease. Things may be okay after all.

No one following, you find the gate and try to relax before the flight.

The loudspeaker disturbs your rest and suddenly your deepest fear surfaces as the airline attendant announces, "We have a completely sold-out flight today. Since there is limited overhead storage space, we will be happy to check your bag now at the counter."

Augh! They saw you! You and your over-stuffed 18-wheel deluxe carry-on. Honestly, what do you have in there? I can go to Europe for two weeks in a suitcase half that size.

The attendant is kind, yet firmly encourages passengers to check their bags now, before they board, only to discover there is no more room for luggage. She even promotes "priority handling" of said baggage, meaning your bag will reach the carousel before my bag, even though I checked mine ages ago at the check-in counter.

No one responds. It's like everyone is deaf. Many suddenly seem to have urgent phone calls, as they are all on cell phones in the hopes that this will provide them a "cloak of invisibility."

The attendant scans your boarding pass, and you hope she can't see the steamer trunk you are pulling behind you. Not to mention a computer bag.

I follow you down the jet-way. Another airline attendant is there, again offering the opportunity to unburden yourself of your bag. The offer of priority handling remains, and this time she sweetens the deal by offering to do your laundry too. Free ironing! Take her up on it, for heaven's sake!

Without making eye contact you shake your head "no." Can't possibly let this baby out of your sight, huh? What do you have in there—the Ark of the Covenant?

The attendant shakes her head as I pass. She is probably wondering how many people will get injured as you try to maneuver that thing down the aisle.

As you reach your seat I can see the panic in your face as you realize the attendants were speaking the truth. There is no overhead space available! Frantic, you head toward the back of the plane, opening bins in search of a spot for your trunk.

"I'm sorry, but all the bins are full. You will have to take your bag to the front of the plane so we can check it."

Like we asked you a million times, is what I'm sure the attendant would like to say. It's definitely what I want to say.

Now my fellow passengers and I have to back up to let you by, squeezing into the rows of other passengers or sitting on their laps to get out of your way. Why, oh why, didn't you do this in the first place? What on earth made you think a bag that large had any place inside the cabin? Is this your first airplane trip?

You return to your seat looking panicked without the security of your case. The attendant assures you it will be okay.

I hear others joking that they will never check their bags, as they sit with their knees up to their chest because their "stuff" is crammed under the seat and on the floor in front of them, taking up valuable leg room. What is up, people?

In my well-traveled experience, reality seems to be that the majority of checked luggage arrives with the passenger at the desired location. At least mine has, including overseas trips where we changed planes. Okay, every great once in a while, my suitcase decides to travel to a different destination than me. Inconvenient, yes, but I have any necessities with me in my backpack for just such a situation.

Besides, maybe my luggage needed a vacation. Luggage has needs, too, ya' know.

Everyone, let your fears subside. The rest of us want the plane to depart on time and your whining about lack of overhead space won't miraculously make more storage appear.

You know, maybe there's a job opportunity here for me. I could launch a "twelve step" program to assist travelers with LSAD— Luggage Separation Anxiety Disorder. Maybe I could write a book and go on the talk show circuit helping millions of people?

Nah, I'd rather everyone just learn to deal with it and check their luggage. Trust me; your luggage will be OK. Even if it does take a slightly different route.

Love It or Leave It

Acing the Test

Congratulations to all the new college graduates out there! Welcome to what is known by corporate veterans as "the real world." We are proud to have you among our ranks.

I've got one more final exam question for you. I know, you thought you were done. Just humor me; this one's really important. Career vets, this is important for you too.

What is the most important consideration in your new job?
   a. Salary

   b. Work that you love

   c. Job title

Before we get to the answer, I've got a story.

Going to college was a "given" in my family. Mom and Dad always spoke of "when you go to college" and "how much fun you're going to have in college." I wonder what Dad would have said if, after high school graduation, I told him "thanks for the offer of college, but I'm good"?

Dad wanted me to study marketing. Of course, I wasn't going to do that, especially since he told me to. He conceded to let me choose a major, as long as it was something that would make me a lot of money. Sounded like great advice to me.

As many freshmen do, I discovered that my first choice of majors didn't fit me well. Architecture was a bit too artsy for me, especially the class in which we painted one-inch squares of color and the professor told us to "feel the colors in the squares." Not sure what was in the coffee he sipped, but apparently it allowed him to see things much differently than I could.

Sensing that I was more mechanically inclined than artsy, another professor suggested I try one of the engineering disciplines. A bit more structured than architecture, there was the potential to make lots of money and the added benefit of being one of only a handful of women in the program. You got it; it was the last part that sold me.

Talk about difficult! Lots of math, physics and other classes with numbers. I still have nightmares. But I made it through. The payout at graduation was multiple job offers with substantial salaries. Sweet!

Then reality came crashing in. Much to my dismay, I discovered that I seriously disliked the day-to-day job of engineering. Sure, it paid well, enough that I could buy my dream sports car. But I struggled every minute of every day on the job. Honestly, I was bored to tears.

Desperate to find something better, I took a part-time job at the mall. While working at the jewelry store I had an "ah-ha" moment: I was not bored at this part-time job that only paid minimum wage. In fact, I loved it. It was so much better than my day job that I asked myself, "What's wrong with this picture?"

With a fresh outlook I packed my bags and headed back to college in pursuit of an MBA. At the time, leaving a lucrative job was a radical idea, especially to Dad. Not to mention taking on student loan debt. But I was determined to spend my career doing something that I enjoyed.

Dad came around, especially when I discovered that retail is part of marketing and was actually a professional career path. *Yes, Dad, marketing was a good choice.* Upon graduation I accepted a job with a great retailer and my career took off.

I've worked for Fortune 500 companies in a variety of roles, each one of them great. I've had impressive titles and jobs that paid me way more than I imagined. And do you know the best part? I've never been bored. I love my work.

Back to your final exam. I hope you answered "B."

Money is good, but the happiness associated with a paycheck fades quickly when you are unhappy every day. An impressive job title is also good, but means nothing if you're unhappy at work.

Think about what you like to do. What makes you tick? I get so much satisfaction from my work that I would enjoy it even if I didn't get paid. *Note to my clients: I still want to get paid, thank you.*

Graduation is an opportunity for you to find your passion and fulfill your dreams. Sure, you may not get it "right" the first time. Just keep trying. A life-long career doing unfulfilling work does not equal success.

The same can be said for those who have been laid off, especially those who were not thrilled with their work. What a great opportunity to find something that you really enjoy doing. Leverage your hard-earned experience and discover your passion. Why not go for it? What have you got to lose?

Volunteer, get a part-time job, take classes, attend a seminar. Do what it takes to discover your passion. Success will follow.

Trust me on this one.

Going to the Show

My husband loves baseball. He grew up near the ballpark and every year his family would attend countless games. Baseball is probably his favorite sport.

While I don't relish the game the way Hubby does, I have learned to appreciate it and enjoy going to the ballpark with him. There is something fun and strangely peaceful about attending a game.

Maybe it's being outside with thousands of others, listening for the crack of the bat. Or hearing the cacophony of sounds: the chatter of fans, the funky organ music and the vendors trying to break my dedication to healthy eating with their cries of "hot-dogs, peanuts, ice-cream." Food delivered to your seat! Yep, the ballpark is my kind of place.

The game itself? I know enough to get by. This can be an annoyance to Hubby, who must put up with me asking questions such as: Did we get the field goal? What quarter is it? Why is the pitcher using sign language? Are we going to stay for the whole game?

What fascinates me the most is the succession planning in baseball: corporations could learn from this.

Players get drafted for a franchise, yet usually are sent to something called a "farm team" or a "minor league" team. Like a training class for new recruits, baseball gives the newbies some practice time—time to prove themselves and sort of a "try it before you buy it" opportunity for the team.

If players do well, and the sun and moon and stars align, they are promoted to the major league. Technical term for this is called "going to the show." For ballplayers, going to the show is a promotion to their dream job. This is what they have been waiting for.

I have been thinking about the concept of going to the show a lot lately. Friends who have been out of work are finally hitting pay dirt as companies call them with job offers. They are excited about going to the show, being recognized as someone who can make a contribution to the team.

Some are nervous, wondering if they have what it takes to make it in the big leagues. And all wonder if they will get pushed out and sent down to the minors again with another layoff.

The good news about baseball and careers is that we can get called to the show more than once. The key is to keep identifying new opportunities and push for what we want. There is always another opportunity to be called up to the big league.

Like the ballplayers that get sent back to the minors, we need to remain focused on our goals when looking for a job. Gotta be ready when the call comes.

I'm anxious to get called to the show again. In the meantime, I'm enjoying being at the ballpark and waiting for the kick-off. Pass the peanuts, please.

Dancing With Unemployment

I'll admit it; I'm a reality TV junkie. Among my favorites are *The Amazing Race*, *Biggest Loser*, *Survivor* and *Dancing With the Stars*. *Hell's Kitchen* is pretty good too. It reminds me of some of my more stressful work situations, without the food.

No, I'm not a fan of the more colorful shows such as the *Housewives of DC*, *LA*, *NY* or wherever. And as a second generation Italian American, I'm not digging *Jersey Shore*. What a train wreck.

I like the shows in which the people actually have to do something.

Take *Dancing With the Stars*. A bunch of one-time celebs and people of interest, preferably with little or no dancing experience, who are all sent to dance boot camp. This boot camp promises participants that they will learn something new, tons of clothes covered in sparkles, new shoes (always a good thing) and that, in the end, their lives will be forever changed in a good way because of this experience.

Don't forget the coveted "mirror ball" trophy for the winner. Oh yeah, that's got to look good in the living room.

Here's how I imagine the experience to be. First it's exciting and sort of nerve-wracking, but you're treated well, get to hang out with a hunky (or hot) dance instructor, learn something new, wear fun outfits, etc. Plus an endless supply of spray tans. Who doesn't want orange skin?

My guess is that the newness and excitement begins to wear off by day two. Especially after trying to move your body in ways you never thought possible for eight hours straight. By the end of the first week, I'm sure contestants are begging to go back to whatever it was they were doing before they were sent off to be tortured—even if it means going back to something that wasn't that great.

Despite the aches, pains and nerves, each contestant soldiers on, determined to give it their best. No way are they going to give up the chance to win a large orb covered in little mirror squares.

Each season there is always one contestant that strikes a chord with the viewers. Many times this person is not the best dancer, yet the audience connects with them emotionally. One season it was Kirstie Alley. The oldest contestant on the show, she was not expected to make it through more than a week or two. Yet she finished in second place. Another season it was Chas Bono. He had a lot of negative energy surrounding him: bad knees, not the best dancer, overweight and out of shape. Not to mention the publicity surrounding his personal journey. Each week he received one of the lowest scores among the contestants, survived the elimination and was back in the studio the next week to learn again. Why bother? Because it's important to take a chance and try something new. Chas embraced change—literally—and he did it in front of millions, including the super-critical judges. Sure, it's risky. But the bigger the risk, the bigger the potential reward, right?

Many who experience job loss have a hard time facing the fact that they may have to learn something new. Anyone looking for a new career opportunity has to be willing to try something different and take a risk. No looking back and wishing for the old job, the old desk, the former colleagues.

It is an emotionally painful and scary time. The perceived risk of attempting something new and failing seems too much for most of us to bear.

Despite the risks, we have to try. We have two choices, really: Move forward, embracing change and trying something new. Or sit still, wishing for something that is no longer available.

The good news is that we may actually find something better than what we had before. It may be something that we never would have considered, because we were too comfortable and afraid to make the leap. What's the worst that can happen? We try something new, give it our best shot, and if it doesn't work out, we move on. At least we'll have gained a new experience by stepping out of our comfort zone. And unlike the dancing contestants, our experience is not played out in front of millions.

I am ready to step out onto the opportunity dance floor and try my hand at something new. Wonder if I can negotiate a mirror ball trophy with the salary?

Nickels, Nickels, Nickels

"Nickels, nickels, nickels. I love the sound of cold, hard cash."

Ah, one of my favorite holiday shows—*A Charlie Brown Christmas*. As you may recall, Lucy is obsessed with making money. A true entrepreneur, she sees that Charlie Brown needs counseling, so she sets up her psychiatry booth on the sidewalk.

I envy her confidence, especially since these cartoon kids were all in elementary school.

Lucy was singularly objective in her pursuit—it was all about the money. And who can blame her, really? While money can't buy happiness, it sure does make things a bit easier. At least it buys a few more pairs of shoes.

After all, haven't we all said at one time or another that we can work at almost anything if the money's right?

Shame on you. Of course, I'm talking about work that is legal and legit.

There was a time when money was a top consideration for me when accepting a new job offer. I tried to look at the whole opportunity, but in the end it usually came down to money.

Once I actually took a job almost completely for the money. Not that it was a bad opportunity; it was an awesome opportunity. But something just did not feel right. Instead of listening to the funny little voice inside my head, I kept advancing through the interview process. At one point, I even declined the offer.

Then they offered me a large amount of money—extremely large. With dollar signs in my eyes I thought to myself, *How bad can it be*?

I quickly found out it can be really bad. Worse than bad. Totally icky, if that word can be used in business.

Within a few weeks, I knew this had been a mistake of the worst kind. Now that funny voice in my head was becoming arrogant, whispering "I told you so."

Stubborn gal that I am, I was going to see this through. Surely I was just going through an adjustment period and things would straighten out.

Determined to succeed, I pressed on. Weeks turned into months as I tried to wrestle this job to the ground. Others had gone before me; why shouldn't I?

There were late night discussions with Hubby about my situation. There was exhaustion. There were tears. From me too.

Finally I came up with a plan. I had put in enough sweat-equity to receive a nice bonus. The idea was that I would stay long enough to get the bonus, and then walk away. With or without another job.

Whew—it felt great to have a plan. Usually I like to leave the party while I'm still having a good time. Considering I wasn't having fun, leaving seemed like the best option.

When bonus time came, I quickly deposited the check. Yeah! Freedom!

Yet the frustration and tears continued. "Why don't you quit?" Hubby asked. "We'll be fine." I tried with all my might, yet I just couldn't do it. It's hard to quit a job without another job lined up.

Besides, with years of experience at multiple companies, I wasn't going to cave just like that. It would take more than a few punches by a misaligned opportunity to knock me out of the ring.

Tears, sweat, long hours, feeling unappreciated. The days and weeks wore on. *Ring! Ring!* A chance phone call with a former colleague about another job opportunity. An escape at last! I practically said yes before I knew what the job was. All I knew was that this one felt right. I had no hesitation accepting a lower salary and trading my cushy office for a cubicle. I danced out the door, finally smiling.

I never looked back. This new job was right. And I loved it.

Years have passed since I made my error in job judgment. As someone now in layoff land, my job "mistake" haunts me every time I interview for a new opportunity. I become plagued with questions and fear. What if I accept a job and it turns out like "the one that should not be mentioned"? How do I ask the right questions, and more importantly, how do I get the right answers in order to make a good decision?

Where is my crystal ball when I need it? Even a lucky eight ball would do. Anything to help me through the interview and decision process.

When it comes down to it, I guess we just have to do our best and trust our instinct.

At least I know one thing for sure: it's not all about the money.

The Philosophy of Donuts

I have a problem with food—I love it. And not necessarily the stuff that's good for you, although occasionally I will get lucky and have something healthy.

A connoisseur of sorts, I know what I like. Mexican food is at the top of the list, great steaks, fresh seafood, good burgers, Italian. Yum! High-priced restaurants, fast food establishments or local hangouts, I love 'em all.

And don't get me started on donuts. Hubby is truly embarrassed by the fact that I heart donuts. Some people have spidey-senses; I have donut-senses. With almost laser-like vision I can spot a donut establishment blocks away, without my glasses. I know where the "good" donut houses are, and I refuse to absorb calories by eating a low-quality donut.

While I love donuts, they are a treat usually reserved for Sundays. Nothing better than arriving at the donut shop early to peruse the dozens of varieties with colored icings and decorations. So hard to decide on just one!

Another treat reserved for once in a while is fast food. I choose carefully here too. If I'm going to stray from a decent diet, it had better be good. Lately this means In-N-Out burger.

As I was enjoying my Sunday treats this week, I contemplated the one difference that the good—no, the great—food establishments have in common. They have a laser-like focus on basically one product offering—a focus on their core competency, if you will.

For example, great donut shops usually only make donuts. Sure, they offer drinks to wash down your donut, but I have never seen a great donut shop that also offers lunch. They even operate only during the donut-friendly hours of sunrise to about noon.

For years In-N-Out has resisted the temptation to expand their product offering. They remain focused on their core competency: a great burger and fries.

Since the layoff I have struggled with focus as it pertains to how I present myself. After years in business, I have built quite a résumé that demonstrates multiple skill sets. I have found it hard to narrow it down to one skill alone. For example, do I focus on marketing or PR? And inside of each discipline, do I present myself in a narrow or broad light? After all, I have a wide variety of experience.

When people ask the dreaded question, "What do you want to do?" I struggle sometimes with my answer. If I say, "marketing or PR" the next question becomes, "Which one?" "Either or both," I say. They say, "Can you be more specific?" I say, "What is the opportunity?" Of course this is not the best way to banter back and forth—makes me sound wishy-washy. Maybe I am undecided. It's so hard to choose one narrow category. I guess I'm lucky that I enjoy so many aspects of my work.

The biggest reason I hesitate to narrow my focus is that I am afraid if I get too specific that I'll miss a great opportunity. Is it wrong to want options, I ask you?

When you are laid off and looking for work, it seems like the best strategy is to cast a wide net. To me that means looking at all possible opportunities instead of narrowing my focus. Honestly, I *can* narrow it: I want to work in motorsports marketing. However that is so niche it would fit on the head of a pin.

My gut tells me that many folks who win the layoff lotto have similar issues when it comes to looking for work. When the goal is so big and so important as a job and income, it is difficult to set limits.

Yet I think limits are necessary. We cannot be all things to all people—no matter how hard we try. Just like the specialty restaurants that focus on one food category, we need to highlight our core competencies instead of trying to be a jack-of-all-trades.

After all, we never see a Donut - Soup and Salad - Prime Rib restaurant, do we?

For me, this means thinking like a donut shop, using laser focus when looking at new opportunities. Résumés tailored for each application. I prep for each interview like this type of work is the only thing I ever want to do.

It has taken me a while, but I have been able to overcome my fear of a narrow answer and learned to focus on my core competencies, even if it means a missed opportunity. The point is not to land any job, but to land one that makes me happy and gives me an opportunity to contribute to the success of the company—a win for everyone.

I have learned a lot from donut shops and the way they run their business. I'll even make the separate trip to their store for my favorite treat. I may even bring some to my next job.

Live and Let Learn

Friends Say the Darndest Things

Have you ever participated in one of those "360" reviews during your career? As if the annual review process was not bad enough, during the 360 review your peers and those working for you get a "say" in the matter. Yep, everyone you work with gets to point out your strengths and weaknesses. Great. Shouldn't we just leave that up to our boss? Isn't it hard enough to hear how those above us perceive our successes and shortcomings without hearing it from the rest of the gang?

I know, I know—this type of review-by-all is meant to help us so we can become better bosses/employees/co-workers.

For many of us, there are so many other things we would rather do than expose ourselves to this kind of scrutiny. Stick pins under our nails, face a pack of wolves, Chinese water torture—hey, why not just stand naked in the mall and have everyone analyze our physiques?

Face it: deep down, whether we want to admit it or not, we do not want to hear what others have to say. We know who we are, don't we? We've lived with ourselves our entire lives.

So then what possessed me to ask my friends and colleagues what they thought of me?

A very engaging, talented, smart guest speaker at a networking event, that's who. *I knew I shouldn't be going to those things.*

The speaker suggested that in order to really understand who we are, we should ask friends and colleagues to give us their perception. Just a few words, that's all. I shuddered at the thought. A twisted version of the 360 review, now for the unemployed.

I must have drunk the Kool-Aide because as I drove home I could not stop thinking about her message. But why would I do this now? Am I a glutton for punishment? I'm not responsible to anybody, and I should not have to face being reviewed while I am unemployed.

At home in the safety of my office, I had a moment of courage and decided to be like Nike and just do it. Quickly, before losing my nerve, I sent messages to friends and colleagues asking for their feedback. Within seconds my email box starting pinging with their replies.

Should I open the emails? I'm not sure I am ready to read their comments. What if they wrote something mean? What if I don't agree with them? What if, what if, what if?

I clicked on the first email, only daring to look at it by peeking through one clinched eye.

What's this? Am I reading this correctly? The feedback was actually good! The more I clicked, the better I felt. I even opened both eyes. Was everything people said what I expected? No. In a couple of instances I thought, *Huh? You really think I'm quirky? And that I have moxie?* What is moxie anyway? Yet, I could see the truth in their comments, and all the comments could be seen as positive.

Why not hear the truth, even if we don't like it? It's important to understand how others view us if we plan on moving forward in our careers. It's even healthy for our personal lives so we can adjust and change and grow as needed.

Their *perception* of me is probably right on target. Having their feedback is like a secret weapon to learn from, a way to fine-tune my skills for upcoming consulting assignments or interviews or becoming a better wife/friend/daughter/aunt.

Yes, it was scary. Yes, some of the stuff was hard to read and seemed contradictory to the "me" that I know so well. And yes, I'm taking all this feedback to heart. Even the stuff that caused me to ask, "huh?"

If perception is reality, my reality is looking good. At least that's what my friends say.

Climbing the Ladder

Remember your first job? Mine was at McDonald's. I was going to set the world on fire at $2 an hour! I had a nifty polyester uniform that had to be washed daily since I came home smelling like french fries. The upside? Free meals. Two-all-beef-patties-special sauce-lettuce-cheese-pickles-onions-on-a-sesame seed bun—yum!

My next big break came the summer after freshman year at college. I was a shampoo girl at a hair salon. I spent my days sticking my hands in people's unwashed, greasy hair. Yuck. To this day, I refuse to go to the salon without washing my hair first.

Then there was the summer I worked as a college intern at a chemical plant. One word for such a job in central Texas in the summer: hot.

My first real job, the one that launched my career, was assistant buyer. I was so excited! The position was a huge opportunity to learn how to run a business and was the first step on the corporate ladder.

Like most first jobs, it was full of "grunt" work. My job resembled that of Ann Hathaway's character in *The Devil Wears Prada*. Stressful. High pressure. Always had to be on top of your game.

And I loved it.

Each day was a fashion show at work. For a shopaholic like me, being around clothing is never a bad thing. Never mind that my colleagues and I didn't make much money, worked long hours and had no social life. It was a "status" job and would lead to better opportunities. We spent long hours at work proving ourselves worthy in hopes of taking the next step up the corporate ladder.

I remember being in awe of the executives, watching their every move, determined to be in their shoes one day. They had the easy job, right? Lots of folks working for them, taking care of the details. The execs got to stand at the helm and steer the ship. I couldn't wait to join them.

Hmm. Funny how perceptions change.

I've moved up the ranks at different companies, landing in some pretty sweet positions. I've traveled internationally on business, managed sports agreements and music concerts, met with celebrities and counseled C-suite execs. I've even worked for myself. Lots of different jobs, lots of changes. The one thing that has stayed the same though is the work load.

It seems like I had the wrong impression of life at the top, or at least near the top. The higher up the ladder I move, the workload seems to at best stay the same or in most cases, it increases.

Where is that cushy job I was so sure would come my way once I had experience under my belt? You know, the one that allows for glamorous dinners, extravagant vacations, time (and money) for a personal trainer, golf outings on weekdays? Yes, I am aware that I don't golf; I would learn if it meant that I had the day off.

I'm not alone here. My friends and colleagues are in the same boat. We're all scratching our heads wondering why, at the pinnacle of our careers, we're still working the long hours that were so common when we were just starting out?

Hubby and I have long discussions about this too. Is it just our chosen professions that require extra long hours? Is it a result of the recession, with layoffs leaving skeleton crews to handle all the work? Or are we just ultra-responsible overachievers who don't know how to delegate?

Delegate to whom? Especially if you work for yourself. The only staff I have is my four-legged assistant, and she's too busy protecting the house from a squirrel invasion to help me. Besides, she's terrible at typing.

Guess I'm just wondering how I could have been so wrong in thinking that the higher you climb the corporate ladder, the less work you have to do.

Maybe I just watched too much TV or read too many novels that showed the "glamorous" side of being at the top. Or maybe it's the economy, with companies trying to squeeze twice as much work out of half the staff, and lower salaries to boot.

Apparently I was looking through rose-colored glasses—smudged rose-colored glasses. The high-level positions were probably never as cushy as they seemed. With position and title comes a great deal of responsibility. Sure, there are perks and sometimes additional staff. Yet the higher up you go, the more weight you bear.

Do I still want to stand at the helm and steer the ship? I must admit that I do. It sounds thrilling, despite the long hours and added responsibility. Although I might want to settle for a small ship.

Uno, Due,
Cha-Cha-Cha

"Uno, due, cha-cha-cha ..." she shouted. "Sinistra! Destra! Cha-cha-cha!"

Hubby and I struggled to keep up. We could hardly see the petite woman at the front of the crowd. Thank goodness she had a microphone. Too bad we don't speak Italian.

"Uno, due, girarsi!" I heard through the music. Luckily, I saw her hand/arm motion, spinning above her head. "Turn around!" I shouted at Hubby. "We're supposed to face the other way."

It was a beautiful, sunny day on the ship. Hubby and I went on one of our adventure trips, this time a cruise of the Western Mediterranean, visiting ports in Spain, Portugal and Morocco. *Yes, it's possible to travel while unemployed/underemployed.*
Always up for fun and excitement, we decided to participate in the cha-cha lessons on the pool deck.

I'm pretty sure the group we were traveling with thought we were nuts. Of course, they probably thought that before we began the Italian cha-cha lesson.

Determined to learn the dance so we could show off our skills in the disco later that night (we heard there was a prize, which I'm sure was a free scoop of gelato) we tried our best. While we may have missed some of the finer points due to our limited knowledge of Italian, we danced a mean cha-cha.

At least the Italians were smiling at us. We prefer to think they were encouraging us, not laughing at us.

Hubby and I like traveling to distant points, where language is sometimes tricky. This was an entirely new experience. Out of 2,300 passengers on our ship, only 90 of us had English as our native language—and very few in this group were Americans.

Announcements on the ship were made in Italian first; the other languages followed. This was cultural nirvana—the chance to interact with a variety of languages and attempt to converse.

Hubby and I try to learn at least a few phrases of the native language wherever we go. Our goal is to fit in with the culture as much as possible, using and learning more phrases during our visit. Still, sometimes the barrier is just too much.

Take our last trip to Rome with some dear friends. All of us had previously traveled to Italy, so we felt confident of our ability to at least order in a restaurant. Easy, no? No. An order of pasta for one friend, pizza for another, Hubby ordered a meat dish and I ordered salad. "Si," we tell our waiter. "Con il pane, per favore," (with bread, please). That's what we want for lunch. In the states, this would be simple.

I'm not sure which dish came out first, but it didn't matter. The waiter seemed to be under the impression that we wanted to eat individually, each one finishing his or her meal before he brought out the next dish. After about twenty minutes, three of them arrived. My salad was still MIA.

"Sir," my friend said, "Ensalata mista, per favore."

"Yes, we are aware of her salad," said the waiter. *Okay, so if you're aware of it, where is it?*

"Grazi," we replied. He smiled and left.

This Italian version of "who's on first" went on for quite some time. What should have been a 45-minute lunch took us almost two hours, with us asking about the salad and the waiter telling us he was aware.

We had fun with this tale throughout the trip and reference it to this day. The language barrier became an amusing story instead of a frustrating meal. Each night on our recent cruise, Hubby and I smiled when our Indian waiter brought our salads. He was definitely aware of our need for salad; although I'm sure he wondered why we thought it was so funny. Unfortunately, Hubby and I don't know any Hindi phrases so we couldn't explain it to him.

Finding ourselves on a ship with limited foreign language skills was interesting. We managed, although we frequently wished we had learned another language at some point during our academic lives. It's not too late, but it's one of those things that you don't think about until suddenly faced with it.

Being out of the workforce for a year or two can bring similar barriers. Technology advances so rapidly that if we don't make an effort to stay on top of the changes, we could find ourselves less employable than ever. As an architect, Hubby is trying to keep up with the shift to a new computer program lest he fall behind. It's the first thing asked during job interviews; is he proficient with this new technology?

Unlike learning foreign language phrases for a trip, staying on top of industry skills is serious business. Understanding even simple social media tools such as LinkedIn, Facebook and other industry-specific networks can be the ticket to a new job. Ignore learning new things and face the consequences.

Hubby and I choose to continue to learn, explore and grow, even if it costs us some money. It's an investment in our future employment.

Besides, we know how to cha-cha now, which I'm sure is good for the résumé. Of course we can only cha-cha in Italian.

Less is the New More

I love to socialize! Hanging out with friends is a favorite pastime. Meeting new people is great too. And I'll admit it: I have a gift for gab. Some of my friends say I'm "chatty." Sounds harsh, but I'll take it. I come by this gift for conversation naturally. My maternal grandmother could talk to anyone about anything. She would board a plane in northern Minnesota to come visit, and by the end of the flight she knew just about everyone on board.

This was particularly annoying to me since I was single. You see, grandma had the habit of showing my picture to single men she would meet during the flight. While she drew the line at giving out my phone number, she would inevitably arrive with several phone numbers so I could initiate the call.

I am going to apologize now for never calling any of them. Especially the rancher from Montana. He sounded nice, but I'm a city girl and need to be close to a mall.

Like grandma, I enjoy a good conversation and lots of words. This was challenged at a recent networking event when the discussion turned to how we communicate who we are with regard to our career experience.

First up for discussion: the résumé. We all agreed that once you have years of experience, two pages works best. God bless those who are creative enough to cram their career into one witty, well-written page.

If the résumé is a written conversation meant to tell a perfect stranger your story, it's hard to compact all the blood, sweat and tears of your career into a page or two. What do you mean you don't you want to hear about my first job at McDonald's? How about my ability to recite all the U.S. presidents in the order that they served—in less than thirty seconds? Talk about talent!

Lucky for me, I've got thick skin and will forgive everyone for not being interested in such important information. So my résumé is the standard two pages.

Next on the agenda: the 30-second elevator speech. You know, where you have condensed your accomplishments enough to be able to tell them to someone during an elevator ride? Honestly, how many of us actually have to do this while in an elevator? What about during a road trip? That would be better. All the time in the world, with the interviewer trapped.

Again I'm lucky. Despite my gift for gab, I have been able to work my accomplishments into a nice 30-second story. Just in case I have an interview in an elevator.

Then the speaker said something so new that we didn't know what hit us. We were asked to condense our experience to three words. You read that correctly: *three words*—three key words that uniquely describe us. After all, elevator speeches are so "last year."

Seriously? You want me, little miss Chatty Cathy, to condense my wonderful career into three words? *Have you met me?*

We all looked at each other, stunned. Yeah, like anyone can really do that.

The speaker then showed us her business cards. Three words emblazoned on the front, uniquely and very effectively describing her.

Apparently "less is the new more" when it comes to talking about your career.

Never one to back down from a challenge, I was determined to see if I could do the same. Unable to narrow my word choices, I took the bold move to ask friends and colleagues to describe me in three words. Even with their help, this assignment stumped me.

How about six words? Four words, perhaps. *But three?* Maybe I could just have a bunch of words all over my business card? Confusing, maybe, but at least unique.

As the weeks went by, I continued to struggled, eventually narrowing it down to the top three:

- Communicate—through marketing and PR

- Entertain—use humor to engage and motivate

- Mentor—by sharing my experience

Still want to use "moxie" somewhere, since this word popped up a few times from friends. I also liked "quirky." Not sure how that will translate to a business card.

If less is the new more, then I am on the right track. I am a "quirky Chatty Cathy communicator who entertains and mentors with moxie." *Or something like that.*

Lifestyles of the Not So Rich & Unemployed

Card of the Year

The best time of year for mail is December. Not only are we inundated with catalogues full of intriguing merchandise (The Magic Bullet, anyone?), but our usually empty mailbox is stuffed with mail from friends. Holiday cards in all shapes and sizes, with pictures and without, some with hand-written notes and others with typed letters. It's wonderful to hear from everyone and reviewing the new cards is the highlight of our day.

For our first Christmas, Hubby and I did the requisite photo holiday card that included a picture from our wedding. We figured this was great for those out-of-towners who were unable to attend the wedding, as well as those who were present but may have had too much fun to even remember what we looked like.

For the next year or two we created a photo card and included a brief holiday letter. Nothing wrong with that, right? We were sure that everyone was anxious to read our letter that captured all the details of the year. Looking back, these letters were a bit verbose. And quite a bit boring. I'm not kidding. Even I'm bored re-reading my own holiday message.

The year we bought our house was an expensive year. In an effort to be economical, Hubby and I put on our creative hats and came up with a budget-friendly holiday card that conveyed what we'd been up to all year in a fun way. The year was laid out in a project flow-chart, one scale featured the months and the other showed the stress levels for events that happened throughout the year. We didn't think much about the card except that we were proud of our out-of-the-box thinking.

Much to our surprise, we had a huge positive response from this funny little card. Since then we have challenged ourselves each year to develop a clever card that tells our story without including a letter, continually setting the bar higher in terms of creativity and surprising our friends and family.

Some that stand out include the year of our first remodel, the year my dad passed away (took some creative thinking to convey such news without being morose), and the year that we wrote a poem to the cadence of "Twas the Night Before Christmas." Was it Pulitzer-prize winning? No, but it made people laugh.

My absolute favorite card was the year Hubby was laid off. With the help of friends who have serious graphic skills, we re-created the classic "American Gothic"—you know, the somber farm couple standing with a pitchfork in front of a white house? In our version, I stood dressed in my business suit holding a laptop and the Wall Street Journal; Hubby wore sweats, an apron and bunny slippers and held a toilet brush. The caption was something like, "With the recession came role-reversal." Never mind that I had always worked; people got the idea, and rave reviews came pouring in. Hubby was such a good sport to wear my bunny slippers.

When I was laid off the following year, American Gothic spoke to us again. This time I held the box of "stuff" from my office including a pink slip and a stricken look on my face. Hubby is also in a suit, holding the laptop (he was working again), and with a smile on his face he's handing me the toilet brush. Classic!

We really like to get cards with photos, especially those with pics of the entire family—even the pets. We implore our friends to include themselves in the holiday photo. We love your kids, but in many cases we don't really know them. Besides, it's you we want to see. How else can we compare which of you has aged well?

We are quite competitive when it comes to our holiday card, wanting ours to be the best of the year. This year, we must bow down to some of our best friends, the same friends that helped us create American Gothic. Their card simply takes the cake. It's their son's first Christmas, and of course we expected the requisite "Baby's First Christmas" card, maybe on Santa's lap or at least in a holiday outfit that would warrant teasing for years to come. Their card? A fabulous photo of their son in the middle of a full-blown-cry-your-eyes-out meltdown. Hilarious, true, cute, and it conveys exactly what's happening in their lives—raising a child. Absolutely the best-card-ever.

Of course we have a bone to pick with them: they are not in the picture. Guess I would want to back away from a child having a major meltdown too.

But next year, they'd better be in the picture.

Driving to the Altar

I love cars. Always have. One of my first big goals in adulthood was to save money to get a sports car. A gunmetal gray RX-7. It was awesome! The envy of all the guys and most of the gals, I thought I was too cool for school.

While I love cars, over the years other items have sort of come in the way of always driving the latest and greatest hot rod: travel, clothes and a house. It's hard to believe that a roof over my head would be more important than a car, huh?

Early in our marriage Hubby and I decided that we never wanted to have two car payments at once. So our plan has been to buy one new car and keep one paid-off car, alternating who gets the new car and who is stuck driving an older model. We purchase, pay it off, wait a couple years and buy a new one. We pretty much marry our cars when we buy them, since we keep them for 10 years or more.

It's now my turn to get the new car. Actually, it was my turn last year except the layoff put a damper on our interest in a new car.

Layoff or not, I'm hesitant to give up my beloved Beetle. This car has been awesome and while it is starting to show age, I am not ready to put it out to pasture.

But it's time. We know we have to do this. We've been to countless auto shows, consulted numerous friends, read every review we could find and even consulted strangers we saw driving different models, asking about their likes and dislikes pertaining to their car. If buying a new car were a research paper, we would get an A.

We finally decide to take a couple hours to visit a salesperson we met months ago at one of the auto shows—a friendly, no-pressure type, which is perfect for our nervous scenario.

Off we go to the dealership, both of us repeating the mantra, "We're just looking; we don't have to buy anything." Arriving at the lot, the new cars glisten in the sun. Like puppies waiting to be adopted, they all look as though they're smiling at us saying, "Pick me! Pick me!"

Who do they think we are? We are not that easily persuaded.

We find our salesperson or "motoring advisor" as they prefer to be called—a very casual yet hi-tech atmosphere, which is more like the Apple store than a car dealership. We accept the branded bottle of water he offers us as we slyly grin at each other. Does this "motoring advisor" really think he can win us over with a bottle of water? He doesn't know us very well, does he?

"So what brings you in today?" he says. Nice opener, I'm thinking.

"We just wanted to say hi since we met a few months ago, and see what's new here. Possibly test drive if you have a minute."

As luck would have it, he happens to have one brand new model of the car we're interested in.

Off we go for a spin. Little does he know we can't be lured into purchasing just because of a test drive, especially since we rented the same model during our summer vacation. Ha! We are one step ahead of you, Mr. Motoring Advisor!

Back on the lot the discussion continues. We talk about the new color, the options, the customization, the price. All very low-key, which seems a bit unusual. I have seen more high-pressured salespeople when I'm buying jeans.

"Is this car something that you might be interested in?" he asks me. ME—the woman, not Hubby, who at this point realizes the power shift and allows me to take control knowing full-well that this "motoring advisor" had better buckle-up. He's dealing with me now and heaven forbid he makes a wrong move or he may experience a full-blown hormone-driven tirade.

I go easy on the guy. He seems nice enough. We walk away, knowing that this is the only one of the new model on the lot on and has the bells and whistles we want.

Back at home we do some more research, including financing options. Waking up refreshed, we go about our weekend chores and head to the grocery store, stopping for a quick lunch. Over sandwiches, we finally discuss the "pink elephant in the room"— the car that neither of us wants to admit has piqued our interest.

"There will always be another car," I say. "Yeah," says Hubby, "plus we've got our big trip coming up. Shall we buy some groceries?"

How we ended up at the dealership is still a mystery. We think space aliens abducted us, and we woke up on the lot. Steeling ourselves for a fight we go in, fully clad in Kevlar.

With another branded water for each of us, we view the car, and this time we ask him what he can do for us. Gotcha now, don't we, Mr. Motoring Advisor? He immediately offers us the deal we were looking for. Huh? What … I mean … well … okay.

And that, my friends, is how you negotiate a new car.

Wait, did we just buy a new car? Panic sets in as we drive off the lot. I'm all at once remorseful and scared of the expense, and unhappy about giving up my Beetle.

"We didn't even look under the hood!" I cry. "What would we see under the hood?" asks Hubby, looking at me like I've sprouted a second head. "The engine is covered in plastic casing. It's not like you're going to work on the car."

It gets worse over the next two days. I cannot bear the thought of parting with my trusty Beetle. I sit in the Beetle and sob. "Come on, sweetie," Hubby tries to coax me out of the car, prying my fingers from the steering wheel. "You'll love your new car."

I cry all the way to the dealership. Maybe they will tell us to go away and not buy from them? Maybe the space aliens will return and take me to the mother ship?
Armed with yet another branded bottle of water, I'm shown my

new car. It sort of smiles at me. I clean out the Beetle as Hubby snaps a final photo of me giving it one last hug goodbye.

As I drive off the lot in the new car, my smile starts to return. I think this will be a good 10-year marriage.

Off the Grid

I heart technology. Really, I do. I grew up with it. Dad was in electronics, and we were always the first in the neighborhood to have the latest and greatest new gadget. I remember Dad telling us, "This is not a toy." I laugh at this now since many children's toys are just that—technological gadgets.

To say that technology has made our lives easier is an understatement.

I think we would all agree that the cell phone is a big winner when it comes to technology making our lives easier. How did we ever live without it? I originally purchased one for safety—you know, in case the car broke down. Now it is an ever-present fixture. Email, Internet, calendar, alarm clock, address book, radio and a camera, all in one compact device. It is like I have the capabilities of MacGyver in the palm of my hand.

Lately though it seems that Hubby and I are consumed by technology. We cannot go for a minute without checking our iPhones, even during dinner. Heaven forbid that we miss an email or a Facebook update; the world may stop spinning.

Honestly, I am fed up with being constantly connected. Technology has become a dangerous drug and I am the addict. A former boss once told me as she left for vacation, "If the building burns, save yourself and tell me about it when I get back." Great philosophy, to disconnect for a while, right?

So Hubby and I decided to take a break—a break from technology, from connectivity, from being the first to read about Kate and Wills' trip to America. And we had the perfect opportunity: a week-long vacation to our favorite resort.

That's right—no email or Facebook. The goal: to relax, unwind and reconnect with each other. We didn't want to spend the days lounging by the pool, one toe in the water while our fingers were busy texting, emailing and posting updates.

It was bliss! Amazing! Wonderful!

Okay, who I am kidding? Here's how it went down ...

Day One
Getting on the plane, time to disconnect. No problem! We are technology-free. Arriving at the resort, the iPhones are secured in the safe. Ahhh ... freedom! Let's head to the pool. just me and Hubby, chillaxing in the shade of a cabana. We enjoy talking to each other, taking in the view and reading books. This is the life!

Day Two
We leap out of bed, instantly looking for our iPhones. Where are they? Panic sets in! Oh ... that's right; they're in the safe. *Whew*. Maybe we should check just once, to see if there's an urgent message from our dog sitter or mom? Relax. They can always call

us at the resort. Proud that we resisted, we're amused by other vacationers who are focused on their gadgets instead of enjoying their families and the beautiful scenery.

Day Three

We have begun to shake. Must be tremors associated with technology detox. Nerves are a bit on edge as we see others at the pool with their laptops and smartphones. Why is she laughing? What are they talking about? Did something amazing happen on *The Bachelorette*? My mind races as I struggle to focus on my book.

Day Four

Hubby's on the golf course. I'm all alone to bask in the sun. The phone comes with me, *just in case* he needs to reach me. I am enjoying my book, music playing through speakers hidden in the cactus when "ping" … it's my phone! Hubby must be calling with a crisis of some sort! Car trouble? Rattlesnake bite while retrieving his golf ball from the rough? What is it Lassie? Did Timmy fall in the well?

I'd better take a look. Augh! Hubby's broken the Rule by sending me a pic of himself on the golf course. He's cheating! I cram the wicked device back into my bag. I'm pretty sure I hear the phone snickering at me.

Day Five

Determined to get back on track after Hubby's slip, we venture away from the resort. Armed with restaurant suggestions, we head down the road. Wait, we need directions. How on earth will we get directions without technology? What? You mean we have to—

gasp—speak with someone? *In person?*

After a quick discussion, we decide that directions are a valid reason for breaking the Rule. Arriving at the restaurant, it was my turn to slip. Out of habit I "checked-in" on Facebook. Evil Technology! Who cares if I'm eating and it's delicious, and I'm sitting in the same booth that the president sat in?

Day Six
I find myself making excuses to open the safe so I can look at my phone. It looks so innocent in there. But I know better. One touch of its shiny case, and I'm off the wagon. I spend most of the day in the pool, knowing that cell phones are extremely afraid of water.

Day Seven
Our last day at the resort. Sweat pours from my face as I strain to catch a glimpse of a nearby computer to see if I'm missing anything. *Must-resist-temptation.* Others ask us, "Didn't you hear about it?" "It's been all over Yahoo." No, we grit our teeth in response. We're taking a break from technology.

Vacation over already? As we wave goodbye to the resort, we realize we can turn on our phones. But guess what? We didn't. We enjoyed our time "off the grid." The world didn't stop spinning. We didn't miss anything urgent. And the Bachelorette made her decision without me.

I still heart technology. But I know I can survive without it.

Oh Christmas Tree, How Lonely are Your Branches

Ho-Ho-Holiday Parties

The end-of-year holidays are such a busy time. There is shopping to do, decorating to be done and lots of parties to attend.

At least there used to be lots of parties. As our group all married and many began families, the parties dwindled a bit due to other responsibilities. Not to mention the drive to the "burbs." Adding an hour to the evening for a party commute is hard for many.

Still, Hubby and I always had two parties we could count on: his office party and my office party. It was fun to know that we had at least two reasons to get dressed up. It didn't matter that these parties were more of a requirement than an option. The events were always festive, and we left feeling a bit more holiday-ish. And the free food and drinks were a plus.

Over the years, we have attended some great work parties, especially my work parties. I have always worked for large companies that hosted big bashes for the holidays. One year, there was a vodka bar and cigar room. Another year, a very popular band played, and we danced until the wee hours. With close to a thousand in attendance, you could always count on someone doing something that would be the talk of the office for months to come. Yeah, we saw you wearing the tablecloth as a toga while dancing on-stage with the band. Dude, you really need to practice your karaoke skills.

Hubby's office parties were nice too, just a bit more, well, sedate. People were guarded, knowing that their antics would easily be remembered in such a small crowd. Even when the company provided a nice band and dance floor, no one moved an inch—they all became statues, frozen in place. Heaven forbid anyone walk across the dance floor on the way to the bar; that could be mistaken for some new casual dance called the "stroll."

The challenge at both parties was always names. Hard to believe you can see someone everyday and then draw a blank when it's time to introduce him or her to your significant other. Hubby and I worked out a system years ago to make sure we were good with names. No, I'm not going to tell you—then you will be able to recognize it when I don't remember your name.

And there was usually some sort of internal office party as well. You know, the kind where each department has a lunch or snacks or a cake—something to lighten the atmosphere as we continued to work at a frenzied pace.

Funny how I miss these parties. I would never have thought I would feel this way, considering we usually had to miss another social event in order to attend one of our work parties.

When a layoff hits, one doesn't consider that there will no longer be a holiday party to attend. No small talk with colleagues, no after-party stories about so-and-so wearing a lampshade on his head. No need for Hubby and me to use our tried-and-true system for remembering names.

We don't realize how much of our social life revolves around work. Just attending meetings or grabbing a quick lunch with colleagues is social. All that ends with the layoff. And it's weird.

It is cruel to lose these social elements at the same time you lose your job. There should probably be something about this included in the layoff packet everyone receives as they walk out the door. "Here's a list of new non-working friends for you to socialize with, since those who remain will be working so hard they won't be able to call you."

We are slowly learning to replace the office holiday party with other events but it's not the same. For some reason, sharing cheese and crackers at the kitchen table while talking to the dog just does not have the same holiday flair as sharing multi-flavored popcorn with co-workers around a conference table—although the dog loves the added treats.

I am sure there will be a time when we will have work parties to attend again, and they will probably conflict with other plans. We will probably complain about having to get dressed up and drive to wherever to see so-and-so dance with a lampshade on his head. The dog will be upset that we are no longer having crackers and cheese with her in the kitchen.

Boy are we looking forward to it!

Holiday Meltdown

Christmas is my favorite holiday. It always has been. I love everything about it—the tree, the decorations, the neighborhood in brightly colored lights, sending cards, the works. I even love the shopping. Just being at the mall, with Santa and the holiday music piped into every store, makes my heart soar.

At least it used to. This year my heart is fluttering wildly as I panic at all that I need to get done before St. Nick arrives. If I went to the mall and heard the holiday music and donation bell ringing, I'd probably grab the bell and throw it at the faux rock speaker spewing the music.

It's not that I don't want to enjoy the season; I really do. It's just that there is too much to do and not enough time. How could that be? Shouldn't I have more time now that I've been laid off rather than less?

We started out strong, picking out our Christmas tree the Saturday after Thanksgiving. We also purchased tons of poinsettias for a quick splash of color. Hubby pulled the lights out of the closet. We were on a roll.

So where are we now? The tree is up, and it's inside. It does have lights, but that's all it has. Still no ornaments. We've watered it, although it's starting to lean to one side. Maybe it's an Italian tree, the Leaning Tower of Yule. Hubby managed to get some lights outside the house so at least the neighbors think we're on schedule. Little do they know that the inside of the house looks like a disaster area, with Halloween décor still visible, discarded newspapers all over the table, a pile of clean socks on the ottoman and dog hair piling on the carpet under the tree. The dog loves to be close to the tree; it must be her way of getting into the holiday spirit.

At lunch Hubby says, "So what do we need to buy for the relatives this year?" I can feel my blood pressure rising, as now we have to contact everyone for suggestions. And cards! OMG. How can we forget these? Which of the 997 pictures from our recent vacation should be included? Augh!

My email just pinged with a note from a friend about a job opportunity. Are you kidding me? Who has time for that right now? There are important holiday decisions to be made, treats to bake, shopping to do and carols to sing. Where is our collection of Christmas movies? Those need to be watched too. No time for something as trivial as a new job.

What is happening to me, to us? The more I think about it, the more stressed I become, to the point of almost being paralyzed. I can hardly move, think, breathe.

Remain calm, a voice tells me. Everything will get done. The voice is soothing, reassuring. I must be having one of those near-death experiences, without the bright lights. My bad—it's just Hubby, trying to coax me out of the fetal position that I've taken in the middle of the living room.

Problem solving is what I do best, he reminds me. So try to solve the problem. "Which one?" I shriek at him—the tilting tree, the shopping, the Halloween decorations, the pile of socks, or the ever-present dog hair? He slinks back, knowing I am on the brink of a holiday meltdown.

Pulling myself together, I realize he's right. An undecorated house is no match for me. I keep thinking WWMSD? *What would Martha Stewart do?*

A bit of holiday energy creeps back in. I make a list, and check it twice. Ready, set, here we go.

Decorations: We'll take the discarded newspapers, wad up each page into a ball and pile around the room. Voila! Dirty snowballs. The Halloween décor is now a non-issue, since everyone will be staring at the dirty snowball decorations.

Baking: I think Oreos come in holiday colors. Check baking off the list.

Cards: We have 997 vacation pictures and only 200 friends. So we spread the photos around the floor, face down, like a giant came of "pairs." I randomly pick a photo and hand it to Hubby, who places it in an addressed envelope. No need to sign them since the picture shows who sent it.

Carols: This is easy; we multitask. Carols sung as we bake Oreos; as we pick out photos; as we create dirty snowballs. Carols sung in the shower, while cooking, while driving. All carols, all the time.

Dog hair and movie watching: We will combine these two into one fun evening. We can use the dog hair as furry tinsel to decorate the tree while we watch the movie. Snap!

Presents: We have an abundance of clean socks. Everyone can use socks. I see some synergy here. Double Snap!

Shopping: Now I have time to hit the mall and enjoy the holiday spirit: fight the crowds at the food court; battle for parking; push kids out of the way so I can get to Santa. With the presents taken care of, I can even shop for myself. A win all the way around.

Ah … I'm much more relaxed now. The plan is in place. Operation Holiday Joy has begun.

And to make Martha proud, we will use some of the extra socks as ornaments for the tree.

It's going to be a great holiday. If only everything was this easy.

Last-Minute Friends

Hubby and I have a bad habit of waiting until the last minute when it comes to weekend plans. We think about it during the week, even discussing friends we would like to see. For some reason, we just don't pick up the phone. Saturday arrives and as we drive to dinner we'll say, "We should have called so-and-so." Too late now, huh?

It's not that we don't want to see our friends. Actually, we think about them a lot. We just get caught up in the frenzy of the week. Lucky for us, we have some friends who are last-minute planners like us. This has worked out quite well, as we can (and have) literally called them from our car on the way to a restaurant. If they are free, they'll jump in their car to join us. They've even done the same with us.

Take New Year's Eve, for example. Hubby and I had been discussing the holiday since early December, wondering if we should throw a party, either New Year's Eve or New Year's Day. We were so tired—both of us fighting colds and traveling for work—that we just let it slide. Plus, as Hubby pointed out, who would want to come to our house on New Year's Day? We are among the few in the world without cable or satellite, so most of the football games would be inaccessible at our place. *(Side note: We have got to get cable at some point. Even the nomadic tribes we saw as we traveled through the Sinai had satellite dishes attached to their tents.)*

So we planned nothing for the holiday.

New Year's Eve-Eve hit and I was overcome with the fact that—again—we had no plans. Zip. Nada. Nothing. The previous year we tried going to a movie, only to discover that people pre-plan their New Year's Eve, and the good movies sell-out early. So depressing.

Determined to have something to do, I bravely called our last-minute friends, offering dinner at our house if they were available. Since my kitchen is mostly for re-sale value and I don't cook much, this is a big deal. They counter-offered, asking us to join them at one of their favorite restaurants. Sweet! New Year's Eve plans that included dressing up for a night on the town. I envisioned a mandatory shopping trip for a new outfit or at least new shoes. This party gal was going to rock a great look for the evening out.

Come to find out that, like us, our friends had planned at the last minute too. Dinner reservations were at—are you ready—the late hour of 4:30 p.m. Late, that is, if you consider this a New Year's Eve lunch. We accepted the offer, with visions of us celebrating with the over 65 crowd. (I'm pretty sure everyone with an AARP card has to eat before five; I've heard it's a law.)

We dressed up anyway and headed out. Much to our surprise, the restaurant was packed with people like us—young and ready to party. Apparently all of us waited until the last minute for our New Year's Eve plans.

We had a blast. We ate and drank and laughed with our last-minute friends. We rocked our sparkly outfits and partied like it was 1999. We finally emerged from the restaurant, full of food and delighted with our fun evening. And it was only seven-thirty. We still had time to catch a movie or simply watch the ball drop on TV while laying on the couch in our jammies. Disclaimer: Hubby would like me to tell you he chose gym shorts and would not be caught dead in "jammies." *Whatever.*

On the positive note—we spent a wonderful early evening with friends enjoying a fabulous meal. We were done early enough to avoid the crazy drivers who decide to party in their cars on the highways. It was the best of both worlds; we went out yet were able to enjoy time at home. And we had time to dream about the possibilities for the new year, including a new job. Yep, sometimes last-minute plans are the best.

Things I Might Do If I had Time

Happy New Year! Another year has come and gone, and we get to start fresh again. Not sure why I always feel so ambitious each January. Must be all the holiday hype, with talk of resolutions and starting fresh and making a list of things to accomplish.

Each year I resolve to actually do something to better myself. Each year the list includes eating better and more gym time. Each year I say that by June I'll have an amazing bikini body with abs of steel.

This time of year my home improvement mindset kicks in as well, and I'm ready to tackle all of those projects that are on our to-do list. Like replace the door knobs, circa 1973, with something a bit more updated. Doesn't seem that hard, huh?

Hubby's in this too. We usually start off well, making a list and checking it twice (still in the Christmas mood). We'll hit the gym, purge our fridge of bad-for-you food and even visit home improvement stores. Architect Hubby will sketch up ideas for us. Excitement sets in. We are really going to do this!

One thing leads to another or "life gets in the way." Before you know it June is here. And I look in the mirror and ask, "What happened?" Depression sets in as I realize that, once again, I did not make good on my New Year's resolutions. No abs of steel or a body that's even close to bikini-ready. The door knobs? Well, we have had this on our list since we moved in—eleven years ago.

Why even bother with resolutions? Obviously I can't seem to make them stick. Maybe it's time to abandon resolutions in favor of something healthier, like "things I might do if I have time."

Things I Might Do If I Had Time:

- Clean the closets, drawers, garage etc. Fully purge, then organize until they shine. We will never have stacks of stuff sitting around because we are so organized. *Snort! I just laughed so hard that my coffee came out my nose.*

- Organize all of our photos, putting them in chronological order in albums. This includes pulling photos off of the memory cards that have been thrown into my desk drawer. (I will know where these are because of bullet number one.)

- Stretch! I used to be limber. This is because I used to be a dancer. There was a time in which I could sit on the floor with my legs almost horizontal and lay forward, touching my nose to the floor. Right now I can sit on the floor. The only way my nose touches the floor is if I fall face first.

- Cook healthy meals. Okay, maybe I start with baby steps and just learn to use the kitchen for more than making coffee.

- Act in a play. Haven't done this since junior high. Not sure why humiliating myself in front of strangers sounds like fun, but it does.

- Ride a bike. This is intriguing because it means a shopping trip for bikes, helmets and the accessories.

- Rediscover dancing. I have always loved to dance. I just don't do it much. This would be a great alternative to the gym, which has become a bore to me. Actually, it's always been boring, but I know I need it so I go anyway.

- Reconnect with friends, even those seldom-seen out-of-town friends. We probably need a vacation; they probably have a spare room. Sounds like a plan to me.

I guess I should include a career goal on the list. You know, something sensible like "find job." Tsk. I just hate it when my responsibility gene kicks in. Better move that to the top of the list. I also intend to laugh more. That's a quick win, easily accomplished by simply looking at my list.

Lots of these things won't get done. I may take steps on a few of them, and if I do I'll be happy, especially if it has to do with the career sector. Out-of-town friends? While I miss you, I'm not much for lengthy car trips, so you can relax.

That's my list, and I'm sticking to it. At least until next week.

When in Doubt, Wear a Tiara

When Bad Fashion Happens to Good Interviews

I grew up in a household of clothes-lovers and shoppers. Both of my parents liked to shop and valued quality over quantity.

The quality issue was a source of frustration for Sis and me when we were kids. We'd look at the clothing catalogs—mainly from the less-expensive stores—and dog-ear the pages with our selections. Mom and Dad would not hear of it. We were taken to Neiman's for our back-to-school outfits. Of course that meant a very limited amount of clothing, since Mom and Dad weren't exactly rolling in the dough.

With about five outfits each that we rotated weekly, we were forced to accept quality instead of the mass quantity of cheaper versions we desired. And little Sis had the misfortune to inherit my outfits, which of course held up beautifully due to quality workmanship. Oh, the torture of having to wear high-quality clothing! What were our parents thinking?

Dad was probably the worst offender when it came to shopping. He adored grocery stores, probably because his father, an Italian immigrant, managed a small grocery/meat shop. Much to Mom's dismay, Dad liked to go to the store with her. He would marvel over the produce, the meats and especially the imports. Mom would always come home with way more than she needed because Dad couldn't resist.

Dad also loved fashion; he dressed to impress. Custom-made shirts and tailored suits were his staple. He'd meticulously pick out neckties, cuff links and other accessories. Dad was a sharp dresser. When I got married, he spent more on his outfit than I did on my wedding dress.

Needless to say, my parents instilled in us an appreciation for fashion and a desire to look good.

This translated into a valuable career lesson: dress for the position you want, not the one you have. I've found it never hurts to dress up a bit more than is required. If jeans are the staple, wear casual black slacks. I always have a jacket, even if wearing jeans, in case I'm called to a meeting.

Unless you're wearing a ball gown and tiara, it's unlikely that you are overdressed for work.

The same principle applies to job interviews. When prepping for an interview I'm also carefully considering my outfit, including an "outfit strategy" for potential follow-up interviews.

To me, this seems like a no-brainer. We've all heard the notion that impressions are made within the first 10 seconds of meeting. That means we're being judged on overall appearance, like it or not.
The strategy of self-presentation, as I like to call it, is crucial to our job search, not only for job interviews, but also for networking

events or any situation in which we may meet potential colleagues.

So you can imagine my frustration when I meet people at networking events that look like they just rolled out of bed. Yes, I'm judging. You can judge me back. Not that it's really any of my business, I guess, except when I hear these same folks complain about not making any connections at these events, or getting a job interview, or if they do, not receiving an offer.

Are you kidding me? Buy a mirror.

Clothing need not be purchased at Neiman's to achieve a great interview look. A few quick pointers:
Men:

- There is no such thing as a short-sleeved "dress" shirt. Only long sleeves make the cut. Anything else is casual. Trust me; I was a men's furnishings buyer at Neiman's.

- Mr. Engineer, pocket protectors are a huge NO.

- Braces (suspender is the country word for these) should be attached with hidden buttons inside the waist of pants. Unless you are going out to slop the hogs, do not under any circumstances wear "suspenders" that have big clips that attach to your pants.

- Gym shoes with Velcro closures are not acceptable. Period.

- Please come to grips with your hair loss and lose the comb-over. You'll look years younger and much hipper.

Women (no, we're not exempt from this either):
- Make sure your outfit is in style or at least purchased

within the last five years. I know you loved it in 1995, but it's not helping you now.

- Tailor your suit if it doesn't fit 100%. Suit sleeves should hit the wrist, but not cover your hands.

- If you're figure doesn't work well in a tailored suit, find a jacket alternative such as a nice sweater. As women, we have tons of options, unlike the men who are stuck with a suit.

- Speaking of options, a traditional suit is not a must unless maybe you're a lawyer or a banker. My sympathy, if that's the case. For the rest of us, dresses and separates work too.

- Lose the granny shoes! You don't have to wear stilettos, but if the word "comfort" was a selling point when you purchased them, they're out.

- Less is the new more—less skin, less jewelry, less make-up. These should complement the outfit, not draw more attention.

Everyone: Buy an iron. 'Nuff said.

Yes, it's sad that opinions are made based on how the package is wrapped. All of us have the opportunity to wrap ourselves in a great brand advertisement, if we just take the time to do so.

There's so much I could say on this interview-fashion dilemma. Right now I've got to work on my clothing strategy. While wearing a tiara, of course.

It's All Relevant

Age is interesting. Not particularly fun, unless you are like my niece who is eight-and-one-half going on nine. That "half" is so important when we are young.

My age number has very little to do with how I feel or think, or even how I act, for that matter. It's a mere birthday statistic, a way to document how long the world has put up with me.

Age doesn't seem to matter to my Hubby either, even if he is five-and-one-half years younger (the half is very important here too; I'm not rounding up). The only time we even think about the age gap is at birthdays or when we are recalling some point in history that I remember, yet he can't because he was in diapers. Guess I was a cougar before we knew what the term meant.

Watching my grandmother, she never seemed to pay much attention to her age. As a kid I remember being amazed at how "old" she was numerically. Was this really the same lady who just rode all the rides with us at Six Flags? At age 95, she would volunteer her time visiting the nursing home to "cheer up the old folks" (her words). How funny that she was older than most of the residents.

She loved makeup, fashion and jewelry. When she was in her 80s she noticed that I had double-pierced one of my ears. Always wanting to be in vogue, she asked me if she should get a double piercing as well. Not the sort of thing you expect to hear from your almost 90-year-old grandmother, huh? *Uh, no grandma, you are good with just the single earrings.* If I had said yes, she would have jumped in the car faster than lightning for me to take her to the mall for new studs.

From a granddaughter's POV, grandma was relevant. She knew her age, yet her mind, physical ability and spirit were years or decades younger.

It's something that I want to do as well—remain relevant in all aspects of life.

I never realized how important this was until the layoff, especially for those of us who have hit the big four-oh or beyond.

As I meet with friends or attend various networking sessions and other functions, it has occurred to me that not everyone understands the importance of being relevant in the workplace.

I am not talking just about clothing, hairstyle, ink or piercings. While those are things to consider (for a variety of reasons), relevance is a complete package that also includes attitude, voice, familiarity with trends and technology, etc.

Attending one such networking meeting, I glanced around the room. Even if we forget some of the poor style choices that were displayed, there was a definite lack of energy and relevance. When I met some of the attendees, it was not hard to figure out why they had been out of work for extended periods.

Me: "What do you do?" Them: "Well, I was in engineering, then I was laid off. Now I'm too old and no one wants to hire someone my age." Me: "You have great skills and can't be more than 45." Them: "Doesn't matter, no one is hiring my age." Yes, you have mentioned that at least 20 times since we met 30 seconds ago.

Of course you are not getting interviews, what with all this negative energy. If you think you are too old, then so does the prospective employer. And your Velcro gym shoes aren't helping either.

Me: "I'm on LinkedIn; let's connect." Them: "I haven't gotten around to using LinkedIn yet." HUH?

Geez. This is not a big technological leap for anyone who can use email. Plus it has been around forever. It's easy self-marketing. *Hello? Recruiters and employers look at the site too.*

Me: "Are you on Facebook? How about Twitter?" Them: "I haven't gotten on the Facebook yet; don't have time."

Okay. First of all, it's not "the" Facebook. Second, you had better make time to join the rest of the world on the technology train as it's pulling out of the station. Or should I just send grandma to visit you in the nursing home?

Sadly this is something I see over and over again. People who refuse to adapt, to shift, to change—to attempt to stay relevant.

For anyone out there looking for work, take a minute to assess your relevance. If you can converse with your teenage niece and keep up with the conversation, you are at least on the right track.

Look at your clothes, your attitude, and your skills and make sure they are 21st century. I'm so sensitive about this that I have been known to cut my hair to make sure I look the part. Read *People Magazine* to know who's who and surf the net to stay up on trends.

Seems to me that exuding enthusiasm and projecting relevance is almost more important than our skill set.

Take a moment, channel your inner teenager, and get a haircut. Can't hurt.

About the Author

A Dallas-based marketer, public relations consultant, motivational speaker and mentor, Tami Cannizzaro found herself facing a minor identity crisis after a layoff. Determined to find the silver lining—after all, there's always a silver lining—she discovered that there's humor in what can be an unstable and sometimes frightening situation. She began chronicling her experiences navigating through this journey on her blog, *Tales of the Terminated: A Humorous Look at Life After a Layoff.* With this collection of excerpts from *Tales of the Terminated*, Tami hopes to provide inspiration and a few laughs for others who may find themselves on a similar journey. For more information visit www. talesoftheterminated.com.

www.ingramcontent.com/pod-product-compliance
Lightning Source LLC
Chambersburg PA
CBHW051255250626
47155CB00009B/3294